PIONEER
Storybook Quilts

Mary Hickey

Credits

Photography . . . . .Doug Plager
Illustrations and Graphics . . . . . .Barb Tourtillotte
ArtWorks
Cover and Text Design . . . . . . .Joanne Lauterjung
Editor . . . . .Ann Price
Copy Editor .Liz McGehee

Pioneer Storybook Quilts©
©1992 by Mary Hickey

That Patchwork Place, Inc., PO Box 118, Bothell, WA
98041-0118

Printed in the Republic of Korea
97 96 95 94 93 92   6 5 4 3 2 1

Library of Congress Cataloging–in–Publication Data

Hickey, Mary.
     Pioneer storybook quilts / Mary Hickey.
          p. cm.
     ISBN 1-56477-003-6
     1. Patchwork—Patterns. 2. Frontier and pioneer life. I. Title.
     TT835.H454 1992
     746.9'7—dc20   92-4201
                                                                          CIP

Published in the USA

Contents

On Behalf of Modest Quilts 4

A Word in Advance 5

Tools and Supplies 6

Making a Quilt Top .7

    Using Templates .7

    Cutting 8

    Sewing 9

    Pressing 10

    Appliqué 10

    Sashings and Settings 11

Stories and Quilt Patterns

    Her Royal Highness, Henrietta the Chicken 12

        Chicken Baskets 18

        Pioneer Pinwheels 20

    That First Summer the Roof Leaked 24

        Lucy's Ninepatch 28

        Prairie Cabins 30

    How in Tarnation Did those Trees? 32

        Magic Trees 38

        Rocky Mountain Stars 40

    The Cottage at the Bottom of the Garden . .42

        Cozy Cats 48

        Puss in the Corner 50

        Sailing Ships 52

    Granny's Puckered Puzzle 54

        Granny's Puzzle 60

        Swallow's Nest 62

    Slapping Prudie 64

        Zephyr 70

        Fluttering Fans 72

Finishing a Quilt .75

    Adding Borders 75

    Marking 76

    Backing 76

    Batting 76

    Basting 76

    Quilting 76

    Binding 77

    Labeling 77

On Behalf of Modest Quilts

I thought there was a big gap in our quilting background—something missing. I felt that too many new quilters were learning to quilt by making bed-size quilts, the equivalent of a 7' x 9' painting. I intended to write a modest little book filled with small, simple quilts that would provide apprenticeship projects for new quilters; and I wanted to tell some mildly nostalgic stories of pioneer period quilts. I made the mistake, however, of introducing children into the first pages of the stories. Having gotten themselves onto paper, these youngsters immediately proceeded to bring chickens and relatives and other clutter onto the scene. It was only with great energy and skillful cunning that I managed to keep the quilts intermixed with the stories.

For this introduction, I wanted to write an impassioned argument explaining that it is important to make some small, inconsequential quilts just to play with the colors and patterns; to say that the basics of quilt construction used to be passed from mother to daughter and have not changed since the first pieced quilts were made hundreds of years ago. Tools and techniques have improved, but the fundamentals of cutting pieces of fabric and sewing them together to create designs remain the same. What has changed is the size and complexity of a quilter's first quilt.

It is helpful to realize that when art students begin to paint, they work on small canvases about 20" x 30". They make many small paintings as they learn to control the colors and to create balance and composition. They would shudder at the thought of using their precious paints and exposing their souls on a 7' x 9' canvas. Even skilled artists make small studies for each major painting. In time, these studies become almost as valuable as the painting itself. They are a condensation of the artist's skill and expression.

You probably understand by now that planning the average-size bed quilt, 90" x 108", is an intimidating job. The cost of fabrics is considerable, and the time investment is enormous. I thought that I would suggest that a small study, both to audition your fabrics and to hone your piecing skills, enables you to see the interaction of the colors and to plan their placement in your quilt. The ideal is to make several small quilts just to play with the fabrics. Doll quilts are such an art form and planning exercise. They spring from snips, scraps, and gleanings and produce gems of color, composition, motion, and whimsy.

The creation of these modest quilts exercises the nonverbal side of your brain and improves your ability to work with color. These are meant to be humble quilts, childish in size, but significant as experiments in composition and color.

More than any other form of quilting, doll quilts connect us with the quilters of our pioneer heritage. The stories of the women and girls from early American days are emotionally linked to our own stories. Our need today for beauty and permanence in the midst of our fast-paced, electronic society is directly linked to the same profound need in pioneer women who had their own exhausting struggle to survive.

I wanted to do all that in this introduction, but I don't have time. I just don't have time to discuss or defend these ideas—the chicken must have a new leg, Stonybrook needs some shade trees, there might be a witch in that cottage, Granny's quilt is nowhere near finished, the roof is leaking, and the town is on fire. We have got to rush back to 1850 and try to get all this sorted out while we play with our blocks.

A Word in Advance

Not far from here, Lyons Creek meanders out of Lake Ballinger and twists and tumbles toward Lake Washington. About three-quarters of a mile before it reaches Lake Washington, it crosses our backyard. Giant cedars and Douglas firs guard the south side of its banks. As the creek reaches the east side of our yard, it splits apart to race around an island. Well, one side races. On the other side, boulders and logs slow the water, and a deep pool is formed. Wonderful creatures travel through the creek: dragonfly nymphs and water bugs, crayfish and frogs. While raising three children, we have examined these creatures, sometimes just out of curiosity and often for various science and biology classes. A few of these fresh-water wonders can be caught with a net or in a jar and examined and touched and tickled. Most have to be placed on a slide and spied through a magnifying glass or a microscope. Under the microscope, the wonders of pattern and light appear, fragile jewels of cell division and of life.

Experience has taught the children that if they scoop their jar through the water, some of the fragile little creatures will crumble apart and quickly decay. But if they lie on their stomachs on the bridge and let their jar dangle in the water, the delicate creatures will drift in unbroken.

In many ways, the milestones of childhood are like these creatures. Fragile and illusive, they cannot be grasped. The events attached to doll quilts are the same. Every quilt has a story to tell, interwoven and subtle. The best way to learn them is to close your eyes and let the voices of the children drift in, to weave the delicate threads into the fabric of the tale each quilt has to tell.

The first section of this book gives you the basics of quilt construction. In the rest of the book, you will find stories and quilts intertwined. Each quilt has a thimble to indicate its degree of sewing difficulty. One thimble denotes an easy primer quilt. Two thimbles indicate that the quilt introduces a new technique, such as sewing a curved seam. Three thimbles mean that the quilt has many pieces and points to match. Pick a story, plan a quilt, let yourself be part of the American quilt heritage.

Tools and Supplies

Sewing Machine

In 1846, Elias Howe patented the first practical sewing machine sold to home sewers. His model had a needle with an eye near the point. The needle, carrying a thread above the cloth, was mounted on an arm that swung on a swivel. Movement of the arm forced the needle through the cloth. A shuttle carried a thread below the cloth. The shuttle swung back and forth under the cloth, weaving the lower thread through a loop that formed as the needle passed through the cloth. Nearly all sewing machines used today are of this two-thread, lock-stitch type.

In 1851, Isaac Merrit Singer patented a foot-operated treadle machine. His machine had a presser foot with a yielding spring, which held the fabric down on a feed plate. The machine was an astonishing success. Thousands of nineteenth-century women purchased the machine to free themselves from the drudgery of hand sewing clothing and bedding for their families. Many photographs of homestead families show the entire family, dressed in their best clothes, standing proudly outside their cabin or sod house, with their sewing machine.

Today, any well-maintained, straight-stitch sewing machine, treadle, electronic, or computerized, is adequate for quiltmaking. Use a new needle properly sized for sewing lightweight cotton fabrics. Set the stitch length at 10–12 stitches per inch. Make sure the tensions are properly adjusted.

Needles

A supply of sewing-machine needles the proper size for your fabric makes it easier to piece your blocks precisely. Size #10 or #11 Sharp needles are a great asset for hand appliqué. For hand quilting, size #9, #10, or #12 Betweens work well.

Thread

Thread for machine piecing may be a light, neutral color, such as beige or gray, for lighter fabrics. Use a dark neutral for darker fabrics.

Appliqué pieces should be sewn with thread that matches the color of the appliqué shape, not the background color. For example, a blue basket handle should be stitched with blue thread.

Quilting thread is available in a range of colors for hand quilting. It is thicker than ordinary thread and coated so it does not tangle easily.

Cutting Tools

Paper Scissors

Keep one pair of large scissors for cutting paper, plastic, and cardboard for templates.

Fabric Scissors

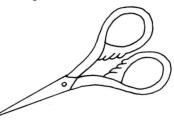

A pair of sharp, high-quality scissors are a must for quilters. Mark them "fabric scissors" and guard them from anyone who would use them to cut wallpaper or chicken wire.

Embroidery Scissors

Use these small scissors for snipping threads, trimming fabric, and cutting appliqué shapes. If you have several pairs, you can place one by your machine, one in your sewing basket, and one on your ironing board.

Seam Ripper

These are small, indispensable, and inclined to disappear, so keep several on hand.

Rotary Cutter and Mat

A rotary cutter will enable you to accurately cut strips and pieces. A sharp rotary blade will cut easily through six or eight layers of fabric. Many cutting mats are available with a 1" grid and a bias or 45° line, which will further aid you in precise cutting.

Ruler

A 24"-long acrylic ruler or cutting guide will enable you to cut the sashing and border strips required in the quilt patterns. Place the cutter flush against the ruler to avoid the distortions caused by pencil lines.

Marking Tools

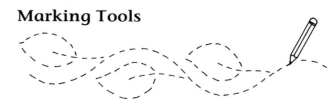

Light dashed lines drawn with a sharp pencil are traditionally used to mark quilting lines on quilt tops. A variety of marking tools are available. If you prefer to use a water-soluble pen, test for removability on a scrap before marking the quilt. Chalk dispensers and white pencils are available for marking dark fabrics.

Bias Bars

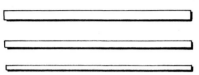

Bias or Celtic bars, often sold in quilt shops, are valuable tools for making smoothly curved basket handles. Hobby and craft stores sell similar metal bars in a variety of sizes; ¼" x 12" is the most useful size for basket handles.

Fabrics

The ideal fabrics for quilts are lightweight, closely woven 100% cottons. Cotton provides quilters with the ease necessary for appliqué and the smooth, nonpuckering property essential for piecing.

Making a Quilt Top

Using Templates

Making a quilt is similar to making a good lasagna. We combine a variety of ingredients in a way that creates something that is far more than just the sum of its parts. To create the ultimate lasagna, we start with perfectly good tomatoes, onions, parsley, garlic, and meat. We brown the meat and chop all the lovely vegetables into little pieces. One by one, we add the vegetables to the browned meat. We must add them in a particular order, or the sauce will have parts that burn and will not taste right.

We do the same sort of thing when we make a quilt. We take perfectly lovely fabric and cut it up into little pieces. We must have the right amount and cut the pieces the right size, or the quilt will not fit together. When we sew the pieces together, we have to do it in a certain order or we will have to sew around intricate corners that could have been avoided, and we will become burned or steamed and will have to use the reverse sewing implement, better known as a seam ripper. (It is a known fact that quilt fabrics are hazardous to garbage disposals.)

To figure out how big to cut the fabric pieces, we use templates, which are like the pattern pieces used to make clothing. The only difference between templates and pattern pieces is that templates are glued to plastic or to poster board to make them stiff and strong. In this book, all of the quilts have templates to cut the fabrics to the right size and shape.

Each template has:
1. The name of the quilt pattern.
2. A letter that corresponds to its place on the diagram of the quilt block.

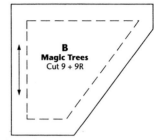

Sometimes, even on a small quilt, the number of pieces to cut is a bit staggering. Don't let this deter you. We will talk about ways to cut large numbers of squares and triangles in the sections on Rotary Cutting and Speed Cutting (page 8). A notation, 9R, as in "cut 9 + 9R", indicates that you should cut nine pieces with the template face up, and nine with the template face down, or "Reversed."

3. An arrow to show you where to place the template in relation to the grain of the fabric.

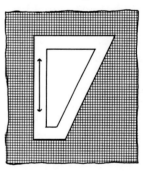

5. A ¼"-wide seam line. You do not have to draw the seam line on your fabric if you are sewing on a sewing machine, because you will place a guide on the machine so that you will not have to think about the ¼" seam.
6. Some template shapes have what appear to be nipped points or corners. These little nips are a great help in matching the pieces for sewing, so be careful to snip the corners when you make your templates and cut your fabrics.

Making Templates
1. After you have chosen a quilt design to make, trace the templates accurately onto paper.
2. Use an ordinary glue stick to glue the paper to template plastic (available in quilt shops), to poster board, or to cereal-box cardboard.

3. Cut out the templates. Be careful to cut right on the line.

Cutting

To continue in a logical order, I assume you were able to successfully choose the fabrics for your project. I measure success in terms of how many days it takes you to decide on the colors and how many bags of cookies you have to consume to make it through the process. (Plan on a week and eleven bags of cookies.)

Cut your fabrics with a scissors or with a rotary cutter, acrylic cutting guide, and cutting mat.

Cutting with a Scissors
1. Place the template on your fabric with the arrow parallel to the straight grain.
2. Use a sharp pencil to draw around the template.
3. Cut the shape from the fabric with sharp scissors.

Remember that your pencil line is on the outside of the template and that the line has thickness. So, cut just inside the pencil line.

Rotary Cutting
A rotary cutter is like a pizza cutter. Because the blade is very sharp, the cutting is easy and accurate.
1. Measure the width of the template.

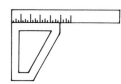

2. Cut a fabric strip the width of the template.
3. Place the template on the strip.
4. Place a rotary-cutting ruler on top of the template, with one edge of the ruler on one edge of the template.

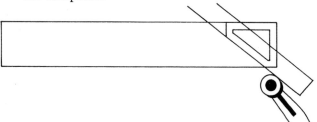

5. Cut along the edge of the ruler.
6. Position one edge of the ruler over the remaining edge of the template.

7. Cut along the edge of the ruler.

Speed Cutting
If you need to cut many pieces from one template, you can layer four to eight strips of fabric and cut all the layers at once.

Many quilt-block designs have simple shapes made of several smaller shapes. A Ninepatch is simply a square made of nine smaller squares. (See Lucy's Ninepatch, page 28.)

It is possible to sew three strips of fabric together and cut across the sewn strips to create three of the squares. When this process is repeated and the groups of three squares are sewn together, the Ninepatch can be made easily and accurately.

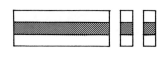

Puss in the Corner (page 50),

the center sections of Swallow's Nest (page 62),

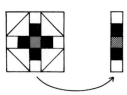

and the window and door sections of Prairie Cabins (page 30) can all be sewn and cut in strips.

The sashing and border strips of all the quilts in this book are easy to cut with a rotary cutter.

A square made of two triangles, as in Granny's Puzzle (page 60), can be made from bias strips.

A rectangle consisting of two thin triangles, like those in Sailing Ships (page 52), can be made from strips cut on yet another angle.

Back to Square One by Nancy J. Martin, *Angle Antics* by Mary Hickey, and *Rotary Riot* by Judy Hopkins and Nancy J. Martin have detailed instructions for quick, accurate ways to sew and cut multiple pieces of these shapes.

Sewing

Quilts are sewn with ¼"-wide seams. If your ¼" seam is a little off, by say ¹⁄₁₆", then a block that is four squares wide will be ¼" off on one side. If your quilt is eight blocks wide, then it will be 2" wider on one side than on the other. If you have ever tried to ease an extra 2" of collar into a neck band, you know this is a little like trying to squeeze a cow into a mayonnaise jar. Since quiltmaking should be fun and a loving expression of the art practiced by our foremothers, you must make sure your seam is exactly ¼" wide.

Most sewing machines have markings to indicate ¼". Don't trust them! Many sewing machines claim to have a presser foot that is ¼" wide. Don't believe that either! Find the ¼" seam line on your machine by placing an accurate template under your presser foot and lowering your needle through the right edge of the seam line.

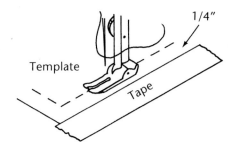

Mark this line by placing several layers of masking tape next to the edge of the template.

Because every seam in a quilt is crossed by another seam, do not backstitch at the beginning of a seam.

Piecing Blocks

When quilters make blocks, they sew small shapes to each other to make larger shapes. For example, when two right triangles are joined, they form a square. When two squares are joined, they form a rectangle.

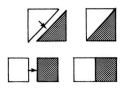

These larger shapes, in turn, are sewn together to create the block.

A piecing-order diagram shows you the steps in which to join the shapes. By following the diagram, you avoid the frustration of having to sew around inside corners and "set-in" seams. In general, try to sew in an order that allows you to sew progressively longer straight lines.

The diagram for Puss in the Corner (page 50) illustrates how to sew a rectangle between two small squares.

Then you sew a large square between two rectangles.

Joining the long sides of these two shapes is the next step.

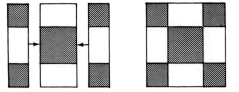

If you had sewn the rectangles to the small square first, you would have been faced with the frustrating task of sewing the large square into the corner created by the three shapes. Avoid this type of "set-in" seam whenever possible, and quiltmaking will be easier!

Chain Piecing

Chain piecing saves time and thread. Place the pieces to be joined right sides together. Place them in a stack with the side to be sewn on the right. Stitch the first seam but do not lift the presser foot or cut the threads. Feed the next pair of pieces as closely as possible to the last pair. Sew all the seams you can at one time.

Take the whole chain to the ironing board and snip the pieces apart as you press them.

Pressing

Precise piecing combines accurate sewing and careful pressing. Keep your iron and ironing board close to the sewing machine. Frequent, gentle steam pressing enables you to see where the pieces should be matched. The traditional rule is to press seams to one side, toward the darker color whenever possible. Side-pressed seams add strength to the quilt and evenly distribute the bulk of the fabrics.

Occasionally, the directions in a quilt plan will tell you to press toward a particular shape or color to make it easier for you to match the points or corners.

Appliqué

Appliqué, the sewing of fabric shapes to a background, gives the quilter a wide range of design possibilities. First, you turn under a hem on the edges of each shape and then sew the shape to the background fabric with small, invisible stitches called "blind stitches." The beauty of an appliqué shape depends on the smoothness of the curved hems on the pieces.

Paper-Patch Appliqué

In paper-patch appliqué, a stiff paper forms a base around which the fabric is shaped.

1. Trace each appliqué shape onto stiff paper. (Those pesky subscription cards that come in magazines are the perfect weight.)
2. Cut out a paper template for each shape in the appliqué design. Do not add seam allowances to the paper templates.

3. Pin each template to the wrong side of your appliqué fabric.
4. Cut out the fabric in the template shape, adding a ¼"-wide seam allowance all around.
5. With your fingers, fold the seam allowance over the edge of the paper and baste it to the paper.

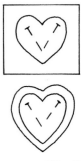

   a. Start with inside corners and curves. Clip these areas close to the paper to allow the fabric to stretch over the template.
   b. On outside curves, take small running stitches in the fabric only. This will allow you to ease the fullness in over the edge of the template.

   c. Points require some encouragement to lie flat and come to a sharp point. First, fold the tip over the paper; then, hold it in place while you fold the right side across the tip. Use a small, sharp scissors to cut away the extra fabric. Next, fold the left seam across the right one and trim it. Take two tiny basting stitches through the folds, including the paper, to hold everything in place.

6. When all seam allowances have been basted onto the templates, press them flat.
7. Pin the shapes in position on the quilt block.
8. Use a blind stitch to appliqué the pieces to the quilt block.
9. Working from the back of the quilt block, carefully snip the background fabric behind each shape and remove the paper.

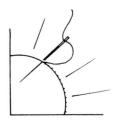

Bias Bar Basket Handles

One of the easiest ways to create graceful, smoothly turned basket handles is with metal or plastic bias bars. The handles for the Basket quilt in this book can be made with a ¼"-wide bar.

1. Cut 6 bias strips, each 1¼" x 7".

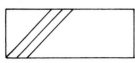

2. Fold each bias strip in half lengthwise, wrong sides together, and press.
3. Stitch ¼" from the raw edge, creating a tube.

4. Insert the bias bar into the tube and twist the bar to roll the seam to the center of one of the bar's flat sides.
5. Press the seam flat.

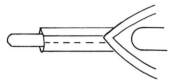

6. Remove the bar. The bar will be hot, so be careful not to burn your fingers. The raw edge is now pressed out of sight on the back of the tubing, and there are two folded edges to appliqué.
7. Pin or machine baste the handles into position, then appliqué in place.

8. After you have appliquéd the handles, remove the pins or basting stitches. Pluck open a few stitches of the quilt-block seams and tuck the raw ends of the handles through the opening.

Sashings and Settings

Sashing pieces are the strips of fabric that separate blocks. Usually, you sew short pieces between the blocks to make rows. Then, you sew longer pieces between the rows to form the quilt top. Sometimes, the sashing pieces are the same color as the background fabric of the blocks, as in Sailing Ships (page 53), and sometimes, they are a different color. In the Magic Trees quilt (page 39), the vertical sashings are the color of the background fabric, and the horizontal sashings are a contrasting fabric.

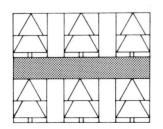

Lucy's Ninepatch (page 28) and Puss in the Corner (page 50) are quilts that have a solid-colored block between each pieced block. This type of quilt needs this open space to form its chain pattern.

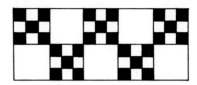

When blocks are placed with their corners pointing toward the outer edges of the quilt, they are called "on point."

To sew these into a square or rectangular quilt top, you must sew squares between the blocks and triangles to the outer parts of the blocks. These are called "set squares" and "set triangles" or "side triangles." The blocks of the Swallow's Nest (page 62), Pioneer Pinwheels (page 20), and Rocky Mountain Stars (page 40) are set together with set squares and triangles.

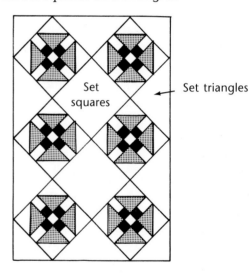

Set squares

Set triangles

The setting pieces are the same for all three quilts, and the templates for these pieces are on page 23. The Chicken Baskets quilt (page 18) is made with smaller set squares and triangles. When you are using this type of setting, the set pieces and blocks are sewn in diagonal rows, and then the rows are sewn together to form the quilt top.

Sometimes, quilt blocks are sewn directly to each other, as in the Zephyr quilt (page 70). Notice that the blocks are given a quarter turn before they are placed next to each other, creating an interesting secondary pattern.

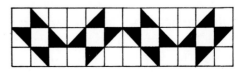

Her Royal Highness, Henrietta the Chicken

by Mary Hickey

"There's Papa," Hans yelled. "He's comin' up over that hill now."

"Stand back from the edge of the platform, Hans." Mama shaded her eyes and searched the road for Papa's wagon. Five months of waiting in Minnesota and five days of train travel across Canada had made Mama's voice sharper than usual.

White clouds billowed across the Canadian sky as Papa's wagon lumbered up Front Street to the dingy train station in Yeager, British Columbia. Hans and I bounced and wiggled while Mama held our heavy baby, Nils. Papa had filed for a homestead on a quarter section of land in the Bella Coola Valley. According to law, he had to be living on the land within six months of filing his claim. After living on the land for five years, Papa would own it. So Papa and my older brother, Sven, had rented half of a box car, loaded it with our cows and horses and all our other possessions, and come out to British Columbia in late March to build a cabin and put in a crop of hay.

I was only nine when we came to British Columbia, yet the move and events of that first winter are clear in my mind. Whether from hearing my mother and father tell about them or from my memory, I don't know. What I do know is that, for me, the courage to survive that first fearsome winter came from Henrietta, my chicken.

After nearly five months of lonely "batching," Papa was all smiles as he arranged our satchels and bundles next to the winter supplies stacked in the back of the wagon. With hugs and grins, he hefted Hans and me up next to the dusty cases. Sven vaulted up beside us. Mama, holding the squirming baby, climbed onto the wooden seat next to Papa. Three of the freight cases started clucking and scolding as we bumped and lumbered along the rutted road. I carefully arranged a little quilt Granny had made for me around Lizzie's legs. Lizzie's soft muslin body felt safe and familiar in this new country. I traced my finger over the names of my Granny and aunts and cousins, inked along the handles of the tiny baskets on the cherished quilt.

"Looks like you got your old job back, Marta," Sven said grinning at me. "Papa bought some hens and roosters today."

On a farm, when you have done a job once, it is yours forever. I had been caring for our chickens since I was four.

"Do we have a barn or a chicken coop?" I asked.

"You'll see soon enough," said Sven with his teasing twinkle.

"Are there bears and wolves?" Hans asked with eager hope in his eyes. I hugged Lizzie and thought about all the stories I had heard about living in the wilderness.

At first, the scenery made me breathless. Soft grasses on the hillsides and along the valley floor riffled in the gentle winds. Blue lupines and wild daisies dotted the hills. Giant cedars, Douglas firs, and hemlocks bobbed and bowed all around. Beyond the trees, range upon range of enormous mountains arched majestically toward a shimmering sky. We saw not one other living soul. In the shade of a quaking aspen grove, we ate the hunks of venison and plums that Papa had brought. Papa and Mama and little Nils rested while Hans, Sven, and I waded, cooling our toes on the smooth stones in a nearby brook.

We climbed back into the wagon and drove on for some miles. When we were nearing our homestead, deep purple shadows washed the valley, and the sinking sun brushed a thousand scarlet-and-pink feathered clouds behind the highest range of the snow-crusted mountains. Summer dark comes late in the northern latitudes, and it was after ten o'clock when we approached the little cabin Papa and Sven had built for us.

The cabin had two rooms. I was glad to see our old iron cookstove with its high, curved legs. The brown birds and leafy vines twisting around its enameled doors looked friendly and cheerful at one end of the big room. Our red table and chairs sat near the stove. A rocker and another table with a lamp and a shelf of books stood near the front door. The room smelled of cedar and wood smoke. I searched anxiously for a bed where Sven, Hans, and I could sleep. The big bed where Mama and Papa would sleep stood in one room, with the baby's little crib nearby. But there seemed to be no bed for us children.

"Papa, where will we sleep?" I asked anxiously.

"Oh, I forgot all about beds for you youngsters!" said Papa, smacking his hand to his forehead. "Well, I guess you can just sleep in these dish cupboards." He pointed to two sets of double doors in the wall that separated the main room from the bedroom.

The doors were about waist high with a pair of red knobs in the center. I held my breath as I pulled on the knobs, wondering how we could sleep in there without breaking all the dishes. But there, inside the cupboard, was a bed for me. On the shelf, Papa had spread my beautiful Pinwheel quilt on top of a fresh straw mattress. The other set of doors held a bed for Hans and Sven. Two small, side-by-side drawers and two large drawers were built into the wall under each cupboard. Tenderly, I arranged Lizzie on my bed and covered her with her Basket quilt. "I think we're going to like it here, Lizzie," I whispered.

In the morning, I could see that Papa had made the log cabin in the sturdy Scandinavian style. He had flat-cut the two sides of the large logs and then cut away an arch in the bottom of

each log. The arch fit perfectly over the rounded top of the log underneath it. This way, the house would stay warm and dry in the bitter storms of the Canadian winter.

Here in the north, where blizzards were frequent winter visitors, barns were attached to the house and reached by a door from the kitchen. With all the work of haying, building the cabin, and caring for the animals, Papa had not quite finished the roof of the barn. The ridge pole had a layer of boards extending to the outer walls, but the cedar shingles for the roof were stacked in the yard. The roomy barn had stalls for two milk cows, six sheep, four draft horses, and two saddle horses. At the end attached to the house, he had built nesting boxes for the chickens.

Hans and I spent the morning unpacking cases and arranging dishes and supplies for Mama. All through the long morning and early afternoon, we carried and shelved and unpacked and arranged until, at last, about three o'clock, we had things straightened around to Mama's satisfaction.

"Marta and Hans, you go outdoors and don't wake the baby." Hans loped off toward the creek and woods. I went around the side of the cabin to the chicken yard and there, for the first time, I met Henrietta.

I scooped a can full of feed into my apron. Taking a fist full of seeds and swinging my arm in an arc across the front of me, I scattered the seeds to the excited chickens.

I had always liked chickens. I found them to be eager, without the gulping stupidity of turkeys. But until I met Henrietta, I had always felt that all chickens were pretty much the same.

Henrietta had a striking, almost human personality. Unlike our white leghorns and Rhode Island reds, she was our only Buff Orpington, a dignified and high-minded breed. Henrietta, on first appearance, gave the impression of being overwhelmingly aristocratic. Above her bright eyes, the skin was pinched up into two little points so that she appeared to have her eyebrows raised in a markedly haughty attitude. Her red comb sat regally on her tiny head. Her arched beak added to her royal appearance. Combine this with her purposeful prancing walk and her continual scornful "tsk, tsking," and you began to feel that she was tolerating your presence with pitying disdain. I could see Henrietta was going to be good entertainment.

Settling in on a new farm takes a few weeks. Mama made curtains and painted beautiful Norwegian-style birds and flowers on the corner posts in the house. I helped her with the household chores and took care of the chickens. We had thirty-six hens and two roosters. I stuffed straw into the nesting boxes in the barn so the eggs wouldn't roll away when the chickens laid them. For my eighth birthday, Mama had made me a split-oak basket for collecting the eggs.

Each morning, when I let the chickens out of the barn, Henrietta would lead the clucking procession out to nip at the tender, dew-coated grass and check for tasty bugs. Once a day, I flung grain onto the ground for them to peck. Mama gave me our broken dishes and the bones from the deer Papa had killed. With an old piece of iron, I pounded these to make a gravel to mix with the grain, for chickens have to have grit to digest their food.

Early in September, on a Sunday afternoon, two Swedish families rode over from the other end of the valley to welcome us. Trailing behind them came the four Oleson brothers and a shy, pretty girl. Her name was Esther Borgson. She had on a clean, white pinafore, and her waist-length, wheat-colored braids were tied with blue ribbons, but the ends hung free and curled below the ribbons. I wanted to talk to her, but I could think of nothing to say, so Esther and I trailed along behind the mothers. We listened to them talk and fuss over the baby while the Oleson boys went outdoors with Hans. I showed Esther the little quilt that I had carried with Lizzie from Minnesota. She liked the pretty Basket pattern, formed by the triangles and squares, and wanted to know all

about Granny and Aunt Joanna and my cousins, Amelia and Carrie, whom we had left so far away. They all seemed close and real when we read their names from the quilt.

Suddenly, we heard a terrific commotion in the chicken yard. Esther and I raced around just in time to see Henrietta flap and flutter up to the roof of the barn, and one of the Oleson boys scramble across the top of the roof to frighten her back down into the center of his tormenting brothers. My heart blistered with rage. How could they tease such an obviously superior chicken?

"Stop that!" I screamed, flinging a fist full of feed at them. The tiny pellets surprised and stung them. I scooped Henrietta into my apron with one hand and flung fists full of dirt and feed at them with the other. Esther grabbed a hay rake and chased them with the tines pointing right at their back pockets. The boys, startled by so much ferocity, plunged into the woods. Henrietta gazed after the boys with withering scorn.

"Always, those boys make me so angry. It is the oldest one who is so mean. The others are only so bad when he is around," said Esther with her slight accent.

"Why would they do that to Henrietta, of all chickens?" I asked. "She is so smart and our best egg layer."

"Probably because they saw she was smarter than them," Esther said, laughing.

"They looked pretty funny running from your rake, Esther," I said.

"Oh! It felt so good to chase them for once," said Esther. Esther and I sat on a haystack and talked the rest of the afternoon. Before she went home, I gave her some pink triangles and squares to piece a Basket block, and she tucked one of her beautiful blue hair ribbons into my hand.

After her rescue, Henrietta took to following

me when I herded the cows out to the meadow in the morning. During her stroll in the grass, she would eat several beaks full of grasshoppers and nibble up any stray slugs. Then, she wanted a nice chat. She would sit beside me on a log and visit, clucking and tsking at a great rate, as long as I would cluck back at her. I pretended she was Esther, and we had long heart-to-heart talks. When the shadows lengthened, I would carry her under my arm and drive the cows home.

Winter came early to the Bella Coola Valley that year of 1909. It struck with such force and savagery that even the old-timers were astonished. It started with a hailstorm early one October afternoon. Purple clouds suddenly rushed out of the northwest.

"Hurry out and bring me an arm full of dry logs, Marta. Then, hustle the chickens into the barn before it starts to rain," Mama said.

The storm came on fast, and I was still at the log pile when lightning and thunder began to rock the valley. I ran for the cabin at the same time Gus, our border collie, came flying around the corner and dived for the door. I stepped over him and set the logs down by the stove. And then, the sky seemed to break wide open. Rain and hail poured out, crashing on the roof with a deafening roar. We could see the constant bolts of greenish blue lightning, but the hail made so much noise on the roof we could not hear the thunder.

Five minutes seems like a short time when you are at a picnic or a party, but it is an eternity when you are waiting for the fury of a hailstorm to let up. The storm stopped as suddenly as it had started. Mama and I flung on our wraps and ran out to find the chickens. All across the valley, hail and water sloshed by in a foot-deep flood, and wide drifts of hail stood against the cabin and barn. A strong wind was blowing, and it was colder by fifty degrees than it had been an hour before. The icy water numbed our legs as we

sloshed out to the chickens. Most of the poor chickens were floating on top of the water. The few that were still standing were so cold and wet that, by the time we had them all gathered into a tub, they were stretched out flat, drenched, and barely alive. We rushed them into the cabin. Mama threw several logs into the stove to heat up the fire. We spread the little stiff chickens out on the oven door and on the bench and chairs around the stove. In a little while, most of them were on their feet again, chirping forlornly. Henrietta stood on her chair, pecking at the feathers plastered on her skin. She reminded me of an embarrassed lady trying to pull down her petticoats to cover her bony legs. She noticed me giggling at her and turned haughtily to face the wall. Then, even Mama started to chuckle.

By the time we had revived the chickens, pale, watery sunlight was filtering down onto the bare, beaten yard. The barnyard looked like it had been trampled by hundreds of horses. The puddles were starting to freeze.

Papa, Sven, and Hans had taken refuge from the hail by staying under a grove of tall cedars. Late in the afternoon, when they came trotting across the meadow, their breath puffed out in white clouds. By sundown, the frosty air formed patterns on the windows, and the frozen puddles glinted in the dim light.

"The boys and I are going to ride up and set out our trap lines while we can still see the trail," Papa told us at supper.

"But that's a thirty-mile ride," said Mama. "That's too far to ride in one day, especially for Hans."

"We have to take the pack horses to carry the traps, so we'll take food and bedrolls and stay at the old cabin at Stillwater Lake. You can handle the chickens and cows for a few days, can't you, Marta?"

"Yes, Papa," I said, feeling proud I could help.

The next day dawned with oppressive gray clouds, and by noon, big, wet snowflakes were flopping onto the beaten dirt of the chicken yard. Papa and the boys headed up into the hills to set their trap lines.

Mama and I were just finishing supper when the wind picked up and the snowflakes started to come sideways toward the windows. Within minutes, it became fierce, howling and tearing at the house and shaking the doors. We were just getting into bed, when the darkness was ripped apart by a terrible cracking, tearing sound, and the cabin seemed to quiver.

"The barn, the chickens," I screamed. "Henrietta!"

Mama held me back as she opened the door into the barn. A blast of wind and snow set the flame in her lantern dancing. She shoved the door shut and held her back against it.

"The barn roof," she said. "It's gone."

Once again, we threw on our wraps and yanked on boots. I hung on to Mama's skirt as we stumbled into the barn. There wasn't much we could do. Hay and straw and chickens were whirling around in the icy gale. We caught as many chickens as we could, turned the sheep loose to find shelter under the trees, and floundered back into the house.

"Henrietta," I sobbed. "Henrietta's not here. We have to go back and find her."

"No, Marta, not until the wind dies down. It's far too dangerous," said Mama.

"Please Mama, Please! She'll freeze to death." I sobbed.

"No, Marta, calm yourself and help me keep these hens alive." Once again, we built up the fire and warmed the freezing chickens. Most of them revived quickly since they were not as wet as they had been the day before.

Soon, the chickens were clucking and chirping. We arranged a makeshift pen of crates and boxes. Before long, they were tucking their heads under their wings and making contented little sighs.

"Mama, we have to go back to the barn to get feed for them and some straw. The wind has let up a bit."

"All right, Marta. I guess we can take a look for Henrietta, too," said Mama.

In the barn, stinging air bit into our lungs. The cows huddled against each other. The wind was still blowing hard, but not in circles. In the dim light cast by the lantern, I searched for Henrietta while Mama gathered straw and filled a grain bucket.

"She has to be here." But I could not see her proud little beak nor her superior little comb. I could not imagine living in the Bella Coola Valley without Henrietta. I wanted to see her parade through the barnyard and listen to her chirp and cluck when I pretended she was Esther.

Mama and I slept fitfully that night. Mama worried about Papa and the boys and the horses and cows. I was worried about Henrietta. Once, I thought I heard her at the window, but I knew it was just the wind. At dawn, Mama let me go with her to check on the cows. We had to wrap our faces so that only our eyes were exposed. The biting air was too cold to breathe without some protection.

The barn was a sorry mess in the daylight. A mixture of hay, straw, feed, and snow was pasted on the floor. The cows had ice on their faces. We hacked hay from one of the snow-covered stacks and gave it to the horses and cows. As we turned to go back into the house, I heard a feeble cluck coming from the cow manger. I pawed through the hay to find a trembling Henrietta. The warmth of the cows had kept her alive, but just barely. Her right foot was frozen to the manger, and her eyes were only half open, making her look more proud than ever. Gently, I pried her leg away from the icy wood and carried her into the kitchen.

"Mama, its Henrietta. She's sick." My tears were freezing to my cheeks.

"Let's have a look at her," Mama said. Mama had a way with birds. She took the frozen chicken and laid her on a towel on the oven door.

"I don't think she's going to make it, Marta. And even if she survives the freezing, she's going to lose her foot. I don't see how she can live without that."

"No!" I sobbed. "She's my only friend. She has to live."

Mama looked at Henrietta and then at me. "Go and get a blanket and hold her in your arms. Your body heat will warm her slowly."

I gently wrapped her in the little Basket quilt with all the names of our beloved Minnesota family. I knew Lizzie would not mind. Tenderly, I cradled her on my lap.

Gradually, Henrietta began to revive. First, she stopped trembling and fell asleep. Then, her eyes opened to their natural haughty look. She sat up. With ponderous dignity, she ate a few nibbles of grain. After an hour, she sat sniffing and blinking, surveying the other chickens like a bored queen watching her foolish subjects.

"She's better, Mama," I said.

"Yes, she is improved, but I don't know what to do about her foot."

"We could make her one. We could use a chicken bone and some leather and make her a new leg," I suggested.

Mama started to chuckle, then looked thoughtful.

"Maybe we could, Marta. I don't know if she would use it or not, but maybe we could make her one. I'll be right back." Mama went into her bedroom. I could hear her rummaging through her wooden

trunk. In a minute, she came back carrying a royal blue gown and a soft kid glove. "I don't have much use for these. They're not quite the right attire for milking cows," said Mama, chuckling.

With tiny scissors, she began to snip the stitches in the lining of the satin bodice. Mama's fingers flew down the seam, clipping the beautifully sewn stitches. In a minute, she pulled out a slender, transparent bone.

"Whalebone!" said Mama. "It will be just the right size and weight for Henrietta's leg."

Tucking Henrietta under my arm, I ran to my drawer and removed Esther's blue hair ribbon. Mama took a twist of wire from one of the supply cases and bent it into the shape of a chicken foot. Next, she cut the kid glove and sewed it to the wire. With a few more twists, she fastened the foot to the whalebone. I held Henrietta still while Mama used the hair ribbon to tie the new foot to Henrietta's leg.

"If she uses this right away, maybe she will adjust to it. I don't know, Marta. Animals usually don't adapt to something like this. If she doesn't, we won't be able to keep her."

Mama was trying to warn me and comfort me at the same time. But I knew Henrietta. She was ridiculously proud of her new foot. She raised her noble head, hitched one shoulder in a little arc, closed her eyes, and sauntered over to the stove.

Mama and I giggled at the sight of her, with the blue ribbon tied in a tiny bow on her knee. Henrietta looked at us, perched on her Basket quilt, and sniffed disdainfully at our rudeness.

Henrietta cheered us through that bitter winter. In the spring, she hatched and cared for fifteen royal chicks and continued to insist that only she was worthy enough to sleep on my little Basket quilt.

Chicken Baskets

Quilt: 23⅞" x 30⅞"
Block: 4⅜" x 4⅜"
12 blocks
1 row of Sawtooth border
Templates: page 22

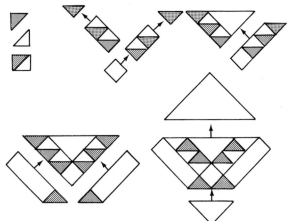

Materials: 44"-wide fabric

⅓ yd. pink for outer border
¼ yd. assorted pinks for baskets and Sawtooth border
⅛ yd. rose for inner border
¼ yd. assorted roses for baskets and Sawtooth border
½ yd. muslin for background in blocks
½ yd. light print for set pieces (Notice in the photograph that this fabric is different from the background muslin in the blocks.)
¾ yd. backing fabric
Batting, binding, and thread

Cutting

All measurements include ¼"-wide seam allowances.
From the pink border fabric, cut:
2 strips, each 2½" x 27", for side borders
2 strips, each 2½" x 24", for top and bottom borders
From the assorted pinks, cut:
28 Template A for 3 baskets and Sawtooth border
6 Template C
3 bias strips, each 1¼" x 7", for handles
From the rose for inner border, cut:
2 strips, each 1" x 26", for side borders
2 strips, each 1" x 20", for top and bottom borders
From the assorted roses, cut:
90 Template A for baskets and Sawtooth border
6 Template C
9 bias strips, each 1¼" x 7", for handles
From the muslin, cut:
70 Template A for baskets and Sawtooth border
12 Template B
12 Template C
24 Template D
12 Template E
From the light print for set pieces, cut:
6 Template F for set squares
10 Template G for side triangles
4 Template H for corner triangles

Directions

1. Piece 12 blocks as shown.

2. Fold bias strips in half lengthwise, wrong sides together. Sew with a ¼"-wide seam. Trim seam to ⅛". Slide bias bar into the opening of the strip and twist seam to the flat side of the bar. Press. (For more information on appliqué with bias bars, see Bias Bar Basket Handles, pages 10–11.)
3. Appliqué the handles to the Basket block.
4. Sew the blocks and set pieces into diagonal rows as shown.

5. Stitch the rows together to form the quilt top.
6. Sew Sawtooth border as shown.

7. Stitch Sawtooth border to bottom of quilt.
8. When blocks are sewn in diagonal rows, the pull on the bias of the blocks and set squares can cause them to change fractionally. For this reason, the borders are cut slightly longer than necessary and trimmed to fit the quilt. Measure the length of the quilt at the center and trim 2 of the rose inner border strips to that measurement. Sew these strips to the sides of the quilt, easing or stretching as necessary.

9. Measure the width of the quilt at the center (including the side borders) and trim 2 of the rose inner border strips to that measurement. Sew these strips to the top and bottom of the quilt, easing or stretching as necessary.
10. Measure the length of the quilt at the center and trim 2 of the pink outer border strips to that measurement. Sew strips to the sides of the quilt.
11. Measure the width of the quilt at the center and trim 2 of the pink outer border strips to that measurement. Sew these strips to the top and bottom of the quilt.
12. Layer the quilt with batting and backing.
13. Baste, quilt, and bind.

Chicken Baskets by Mary Hickey, 1989, Seattle, Washington, 23⅝" x 30¾". Dainty baskets are complemented by the delicate print in the set blocks. A Sawtooth border across the bottom enlivens this winsome quilt.

Pioneer Pinwheels

Quilt: 20½" x 27½"
Block: 5" x 5"
6 blocks
Templates: page 23

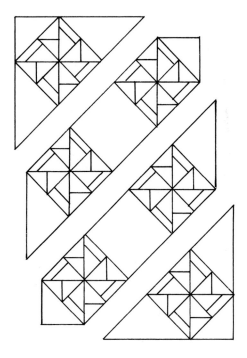

Materials: 44"-wide fabric

½ yd. blues for pinwheels and outer border
¼ yd. peach for inner border and pinwheels
⅛ yd. white for background in blocks
¼ yd. print for large set pieces
⅝ yd. backing fabric
Batting, binding, and thread

Cutting

All measurements include ¼"-wide seam allowances.
From the blue fabrics, cut:
2 strips, each 3" x 24", for side borders
2 strips, each 3" x 22", for top and bottom borders
24 Template A
From the peach fabrics, cut:
2 strips, each 1" x 23", for inner border (sides)
2 strips, each 1" x 17", for inner border (top and bottom)
24 Template A
From the white background fabric, cut:
24 Template A
24 Template B
From the print fabric, cut:
2 Template X for set squares
6 template Y for side triangles
4 template Z for corner triangles

Directions

1. Piece 6 blocks as shown. To simplify matching the 8 points in the center of the blocks, press all the seams open. As you assemble the blocks, pin the pieces to prevent them from shifting.

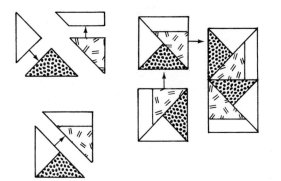

2. Sew the blocks in diagonal rows as shown.

3. Stitch the rows together to form the quilt top.
4. When blocks are sewn in diagonal rows, the pull on the bias of the blocks and set squares can cause them to change fractionally. For this reason, the borders are cut slightly longer than necessary and trimmed to fit the quilt. Measure the length of the quilt at the center and trim 2 of the peach strips to that measurement. Sew these strips to the sides of the quilt, easing or stretching as necessary.
5. Measure the width of the quilt at the center and trim 2 of the peach strips to that measurement. Sew these strips to the top and bottom of the quilt, easing or stretching as necessary.
6. Measure the length of the quilt at the center and trim 2 of the blue strips to that measurement. Sew these strips to the sides of the quilt.
7. Measure the width of the quilt at the center and trim 2 of the blue strips to that measurement. Sew strips to the top and bottom of the quilt.
8. Layer the quilt with batting and backing.
9. Baste, quilt, and bind.

Pioneer Pinwheels by Mary Hickey, 1991, Seattle, Washington, 20½" x 27½". Pinwheels, a favorite early-American toy, spin across this lively quilt. A fascinating print of antique dolls, once a beloved dress of the author's daughter, separates the blocks and transforms this quilt into a cherished treasure.

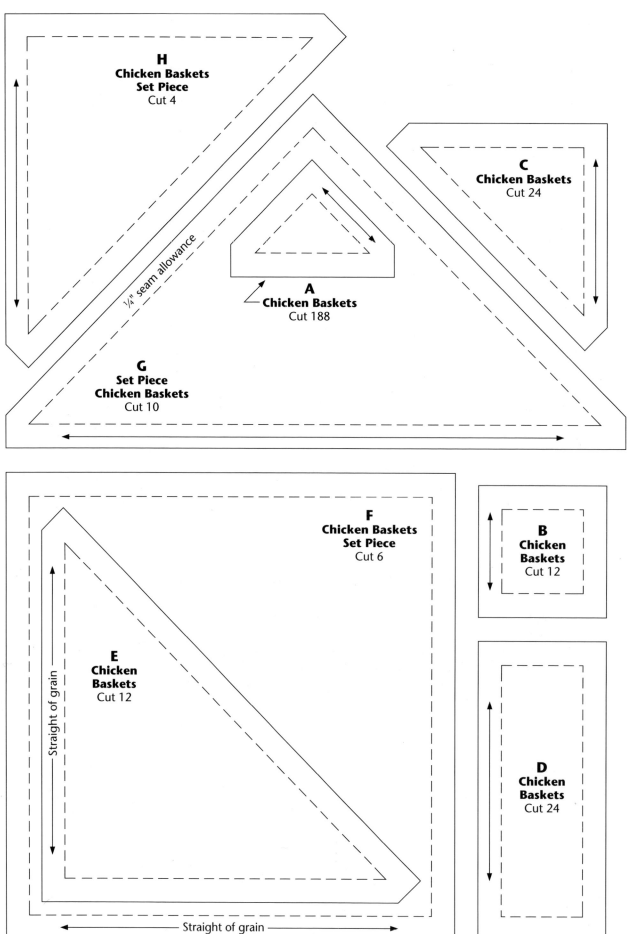

H
Chicken Baskets
Set Piece
Cut 4

¼" seam allowance

A
Chicken Baskets
Cut 188

C
Chicken Baskets
Cut 24

G
Set Piece
Chicken Baskets
Cut 10

F
Chicken Baskets
Set Piece
Cut 6

E
Chicken
Baskets
Cut 12

Straight of grain

Straight of grain

B
Chicken
Baskets
Cut 12

D
Chicken
Baskets
Cut 24

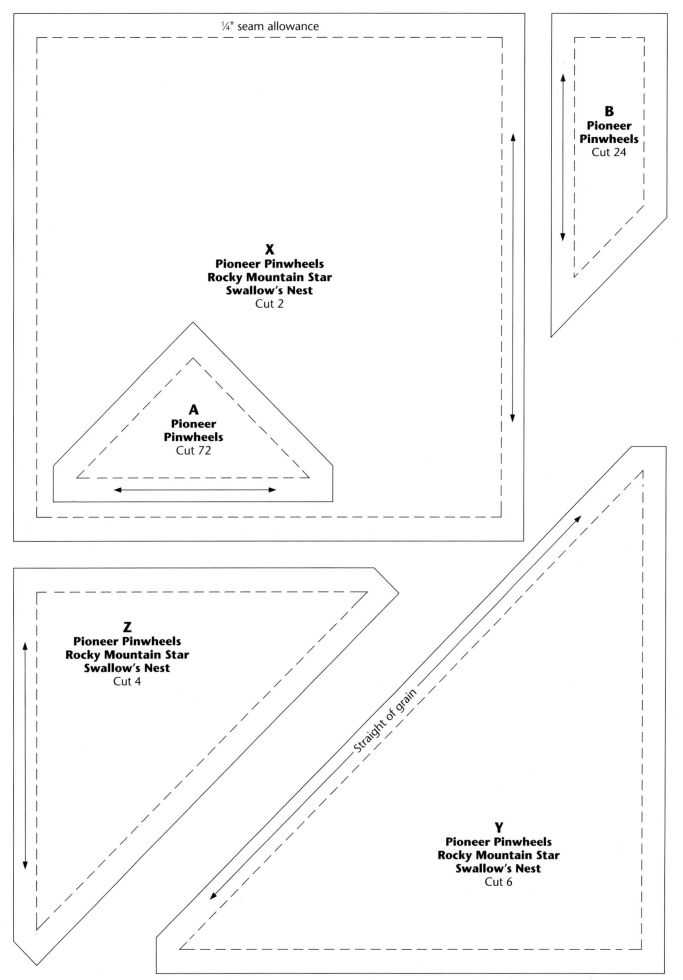

¼" seam allowance

X
Pioneer Pinwheels
Rocky Mountain Star
Swallow's Nest
Cut 2

A
Pioneer
Pinwheels
Cut 72

B
Pioneer
Pinwheels
Cut 24

Z
Pioneer Pinwheels
Rocky Mountain Star
Swallow's Nest
Cut 4

Straight of grain

Y
Pioneer Pinwheels
Rocky Mountain Star
Swallow's Nest
Cut 6

That First Summer The Roof Leaked

by Mary Hickey

After endless months confined in the little dugout, we were like jack rabbits poking our noses up through the cold, crusty ground. The stubbled earth was still thawing, with puddles of clear water licking at patches of dingy snow. Wispy clouds raced across the immense Kansas sky. It was early in the spring of 1878 when Papa started to build our sod house. He had planned to build us a log house, but our part of Kansas was too dry to grow trees. Carting lumber across the state to our homestead would be too costly, so the endless miles of prairie sod were going to be the material for our house.

We had spent the winter in our cavelike dugout, cramped and damp and dark and dirty. Mama had gotten so she could cope with the dirt from the walls, roof, and floor sifting into all our food and belongings. She even managed to deal with the floor turning to mud. But the night a bull snake fell out of the roof onto Mama's bed, Papa knew he couldn't wait till he had the money to buy lumber.

"Well, Catherine, this year we'll build a house of 'prairie marble,' and by next year, we can save enough to buy lumber for a proper house," Papa said proudly.

"Let's put it near the crest of that little rise over there," Mama said, pointing to a humble hill in that vast landscape of prairie.

"I'll start clearing it right away," Papa agreed. "James, after I've dug up the grass, you take that wide shovel and pack the earth down to form a smooth floor."

James and Papa toiled most of that first day, clearing the site and packing the floor. Once the site was cleared, Papa and James started to cut the sod blocks. Our neighbor, Mr. Putnam, came with his oxen to help with the sod cutting.

Papa harnessed Smokey and Sam together with Mr. Putnam's team, and using a special sod cutter called a grasshopper plow, they sliced long, thin strips of sod from the earth. Will and I followed Papa up and down the furrows, enjoying the steady flow of the long sod ribbon from the curved plowshare. Now and then, a strip kinked and buckled into a little hummock that Will and I could sit on and watch as James used a sharpened spade to cut the strips into individual bricks.

My two-year-old brother, William, and I wanted to help, but the work was far too heavy for us.

"It's your job to watch William while I keep the cookstove hot," Mama said. "It takes a lot of cornbread and stew to feed those hard workers."

At thirteen, James was tall and gangling. His sandy hair stood out from his head and bounced as he dug his spade into the unyielding earth. His freckles darkened and his skin turned pink in the early spring sun just as Mama's and mine did. He was a wild, jolly-looking boy and an earnest worker, but he was having considerable trouble cutting the sod bricks the right size.

"If the bricks aren't uniform, the house won't be as strong as the Kansas storms," Papa cautioned.

"Lucy, bring Will and come over here," James called. "I need your help."

By now, the grasses were tall enough to wave in the ever-blowing winds. Butterflies and meadowlarks flew over the budding daisies. Rabbits loped ahead of us as we hippety-hopped over to where James was working hard.

"Will, you're going to be my ruler," James explained. "Hold your arms out. Lucy, you make sure his left hand is at the end of the strip, then push a stick in the sod where his right hand touches. That way, all the blocks will be the same size."

"I helping," William chortled.

I felt mighty proud to be helping, too.

The sod bricks James cut were all about two feet long, one foot wide, and four inches thick. At first, James could barely load the fifty-pound bricks onto the spring wagon used for hauling to the building site, but after a few days, he didn't find it so difficult.

When the wagon was loaded, the oxen pulled it to the house site. Papa and James stacked the bricks, one layer after another, around the perimeter of the building. James developed a system for tipping the sod over and sliding it, grass side down, on a plank. By moving the wagon every fourth or fifth time, the sod brick was always close to where it was supposed to be placed. They put the bricks side by side so the walls were actually two feet thick. William and I carried pans of loose dirt to stuff between the cracks and crevices.

All through the early spring, we toiled under the great, curved Kansas sky. The prairie bloomed into a waving sea of purple Jack-in-the-pulpits and pink brier roses. And brick by sod brick, our house grew and grew.

Papa and James carefully set wooden frames for the door and windows in place as they built the sod walls up around them. Cottonwood poles made a strong frame for the roof. Mama and William and I collected willow brush to lay over the pole frame. Then, Papa and James topped the brush with more strips of sod.

It took one full acre of sod to build our sixteen-by-twenty foot house. With its massive dirt walls weighing ninety tons, our house was a cool haven in the scorching Kansas summer, and warm and snug through the winter blizzards. During the five years we lived in the soddy, it withstood three prairie fires. But that first summer, the roof leaked.

We moved in on a golden day in late April. Mama put her big, carved bed at the south end of the room. Mama's fine walnut trunk stood at the foot of the bed. The trundle that Will and I slept on went under Mama and Papa's bed. James had a cot at the other end of the room. Mama put a pretty, red-flowered coverlet on James' cot and called it our daybed. We sat on it during winter afternoons when the chores were done. Mama bleached feed sacks and embroidered them with cheerful cardinals to make curtains for the soddy's three windows.

Our table and cast-iron cookstove stood along the west wall. James helped Papa make a special table with drop leaves so that it did not take up too much room when we were not eating.

That spring, Mama told me I was old enough to learn to make a little patchwork quilt for my cloth doll, Elizabeth. Mama made her for me when I was six. Elizabeth had cloth hair, and her friendly eyes and smiling mouth were embroidered with colored thread. Elizabeth's blue dress had bands of pretty trim along the skirt. I thought a quilt was just what Elizabeth wanted.

Mama had carried her fine walnut trunk with her all the way from Pennsylvania. I had only seen her open it twice that I could remember. She kept her fine handmade linens in it, as well as a few books. There were some embroidered tablecloths and some beautiful pieces of lace and tatting and crochet work. But the most beautiful of all were the handmade quilts. She had one with appliquéd patterns of ferns and flowers that were sewn with stitches so tiny you could hardly see them. Another had beautiful Basket blocks with the names of all her family members and girlhood friends. She also kept a bag of carefully folded scraps in the trunk.

I held my breath as Mama lifted the lid of the trunk. Her eyes filled with tears as she opened it. I loved the sight and even the clean smell of those beautiful linens. Even at the age of nine, I could understand the vast difference between the hopes and expectations that the linens held and the crushing life that Mama had accepted instead.

Mama and I chose some scraps for my quilt, including scraps from James' daybed cover. She gave me my own needle and some thread and a little tin with a fitted lid for my very own sewing box. I learned to cut the scraps into little squares all the same size, to stitch them into straight rows, and to sew the rows together to make the Ninepatch block. When my other chores were done and William was napping, I could work on my blocks. Patch by little patch, my quilt grew just as our house had.

Papa and James labored in the fields with the plow and corn planter. From daylight till dark, they plodded back and forth across the field, breaking up the tough sod and jabbing the seeds into the ground until they were so tired at night they could hardly talk or laugh. They just ate and went to bed. In the evenings, Mama let me sit with her and stitch on my Ninepatches till the light grew too thin to sew.

After Papa and James had planted the corn and wheat and helped Mama plant a garden in the ground where they had dug the sod for the house, they took the oxen across the prairie to help another family, the Oilunds, build their sod house. They had been gone about four days when Will and I spied a horseman riding toward our soddy. As he drew closer, we ran inside to warn Mama. She waited anxiously in the doorway until she recognized him as Mr. Putnam, our neighbor.

"Hannah has had an accident, and her baby is coming early. Could you see your way to coming and helping us out?"

"Of course, we can. Just let me get my box of medicines." Mama looked stricken as she remembered that our wagon was with Papa.

"I'll have to ride Shadow, Lucy. You and William will have to stay here alone. You're a big girl now, and I know I can count on you to watch William for a few hours while I go to help Hannah Putnam," she said. Mama, a born doctor, was hurrying around, gathering her little store of medicinal supplies.

"Don't light the fire till I get back. Stay away from the well and keep a very close eye on William. You can milk Buttercup if I'm not back in time, but keep William with you all the time."

She mounted Shadow, our dappled horse, and rode off with Mr. Putnam toward the dry creek bed that separated our homesteads. She looked very tiny and pretty as she rode away.

Will and I stood silently, staring at the spot on the horizon where she had disappeared, and suddenly, the silence of the prairie was deafening. I tried to quell my anxiety at being alone in that vast, empty space by doing the most grown-up thing I could think of: chores.

"Let's go get the sheep, Will," I said.

"We get sheep," Will sang.

We brought the sheep up to their little corral, swept the house, hauled in water, milked the cow, and carried wood to the box by the stove. The sun was lowering toward the horizon when we noticed the wind whipping the laundry and angry clouds boiling in the eastern sky. The clean clothes were hanging on a rope strung between the house and the garden.

"The rope is too high, Will. We'll have to get a chair to reach the laundry," I said. I was feeling very grown-up but not very tall.

"I'll stand on the chair and hand the clothes to you, Will. And you take them in and put them on Mama's bed."

"I put on Mama's bed," Will shouted each time he ran in with more of the laundry.

As we dragged the chair over the doorsill, the first big drops began to fall, and when we closed the door, the lightning started.

At first, it was fun being in the cozy house during the big storm. But, as darkness filled the little house, the sod roof began to leak. Will and I put pans under the first two leaks and buckets under the next two. Then, we got the dishpan and the laundry tub. By dark, it was raining in the house. Will's shoulders were shivering and his teeth were chattering when I disobeyed Mama and lit the kerosene lamp. How could Mama find the house in this enormous, empty landscape without a light in the window? As I placed the lamp on the sill, I realized that Mama could not cross the rising creek during the storm. Will and I were going to spend the night alone in the leaking house. We ate some cold biscuits and drank milk for supper.

I did not like the idea of sleeping in a cold house, in a damp bed. Will was wet and cold, and I knew the danger of illness following a bad chill. How could I keep him warm and dry when the roof was letting the rain pour into the house? A little knot of anxiety gripped my stomach. Searching the gloom, I tried to think of a way to keep warm and dry.

"Will, Quick! Help me pull our bed out. We're going to put it under the table!" We pushed and pulled and dragged until we got our trundle under the drop-leaf table.

Will and I carefully shoved Mama's fine trunk to the end of our bed. I took Elizabeth and my sewing tin with my Ninepatches in it and put them in bed, too. Quickly, we changed into dry clothes, crawled into bed, and pulled the covers over our heads. I knew it was wasteful to leave the lamp burning, but I couldn't bring myself to darken that cold, dripping, lonely house by blowing out the oil flame.

That was how Mama, Papa, and James found us just after dawn: in bed, under the covers, under the table, with Mama's trunk, Elizabeth, and my tin, dry and sound asleep.

Papa had heard of the trouble at Putnams on his way back from helping the Oilunds and had stopped to see if Mama was there. They all waited in the wagon by the creek most of the night in the hope of fording it and getting back to us.

"Lucy, to think you just dragged that trundle under the table and kept Will dry through that awful storm. I don't know that I'd have thought of that!" Mama cried.

Papa took the canvas from the covered wagon and stretched it over the roof of the house for the rest of the summer. After the harvest, Papa was able to buy lumber to make a proper roof and a floor. When the walls settled, Papa made a plaster of clay and water and smoothed it over the walls. A coat of whitewash every six months kept the walls looking clean and cheerful. (Mama scrubbed the canvas clean, and we stitched it into shirts for Papa and James.)

Whenever I see a Ninepatch quilt, I think of that first Kansas house built brick by sod brick; and when I see the squares between the Ninepatch blocks, I think of the whole acre of prairie that went into that house.

Lucy's Ninepatch

Quilt: 24½" x 24½"
Block: 3" x 3"
25 blocks (13 Block I and 12 Block II)

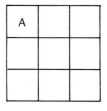

Materials: 44"-wide fabric

½ yd. floral for outer border
⅛ yd. rose for middle border
¼ yd. assorted roses for Ninepatches
¼ yd. pink for Ninepatches
⅓ yd. rose beige for set blocks and inner border
¾ yd. backing fabric
Batting, binding, and thread

Cutting

All measurements include ¼"-wide seam allowances.
From the floral border fabric, cut:
    2 strips, each 3½" x 18½", for outer border (sides)
    2 strips, each 3½" x 24½", for outer border (top and bottom)
From the rose for middle border, cut:
    2 strips, each 1" x 17½", for side borders
    2 strips, each 1" x 18½", for top and bottom borders
From the assorted roses, cut:
    65 Template A
From the pink, cut:
    52 Template A
From the rose beige for set blocks and inner border, cut:
    2 strips, each 1½" x 15½", for side borders
    2 strips, each 1½" x 17½", for top and bottom borders
    12 Template B (for Block II)

Directions

1. Piece 13 blocks as shown (Block I).

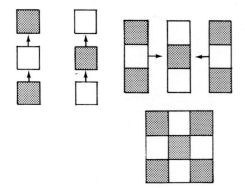

2. Sew Blocks I and II together in rows as shown.

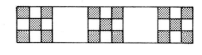

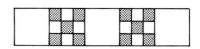

3. Sew the rows together to form the quilt top.
4. Stitch the inner borders to the quilt, sides first, then the top and bottom.
5. Sew the middle borders to the quilt, sides first, then the top and bottom.
6. Sew the outer borders to the quilt, sides first, then the top and bottom.
7. Layer with batting and backing.
8. Baste, quilt, and bind.

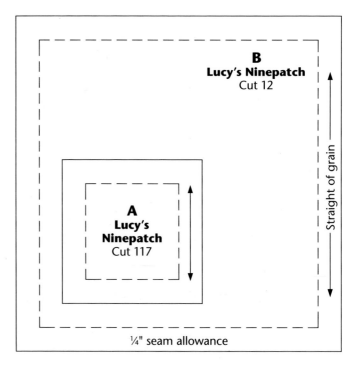

B
Lucy's Ninepatch
Cut 12

A
Lucy's Ninepatch
Cut 117

Straight of grain

¼" seam allowance

Lucy's Ninepatch by Judy Pollard, 1991, Seattle, Washington, 24½" x 24½". A beautiful floral paisley, similar to those used on coverlets in the nineteenth century, borders this simple, faithful pattern.

Prairie Cabins

Quilt: 24½" x 27½"
Block: 4½" x 3½"
12 blocks

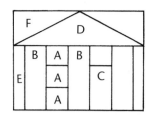

Materials: 44"-wide fabric

½ yd. beige for background and inner border
½ yd. red for outer border and houses
¼ yd. each of green and blue for cabins
¼ yd. black for doors, windows, and roof
¼ yd. stripe for sashing
¾ yd. backing fabric
Batting, binding, and thread

Cutting

All measurements include ¼"-wide seam allowances.
From the beige, cut:
  24 Template E
  24 Template F
  8 Template G for sashing between cabins
  4 strips, each 2" x 19½", for inner border
From the red, cut:
  2 strips, each 3" x 22½", for outer border (sides)
  2 strips, each 3" x 24½", for outer border (top and bottom)
  12 Template A
  12 Template B
From the blue, cut:
  12 Template A
  12 Template B
From the green, cut:
  12 Template A
  12 Template B
From the black, cut:
  12 Template A
  12 Template C
  12 Template D
From the stripe, cut:
  4 strips, each 1¾" x 16½", for sashing between rows

Directions

1. Piece 12 cabins as shown. The roof section of this little block has no vertical seams, while the cabin section has 6. This makes matching the two sections a little difficult. If the cabin section is too wide for the roof section, resew the two outer seams with a slightly wider seam allowance. If it is too small for the roof section, rip out only the 2 outer seams and resew them with a narrower

seam allowance.

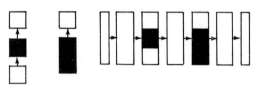

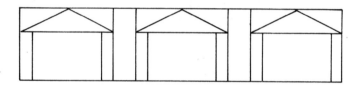

2. Sew the blocks together in rows of 3 as shown.

3. Sew a striped sashing piece to the bottom of each row.
4. Sew the rows together to form the quilt top.
5. Sew the inner borders to the quilt, sides first, then the top and bottom.
6. Sew the outer borders to the quilt, sides first, then the top and bottom.
7. Layer with batting and backing.
8. Baste, quilt, and bind.

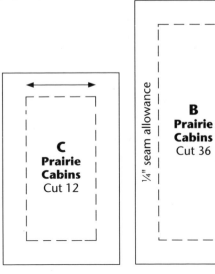

Prairie Cabins by Mary Hickey, 1990, Seattle, Washington, 27½" x 27½". Snug cabins stitched in warm tones capture the spirit of the prairies. Quilted by Helen Hickey.

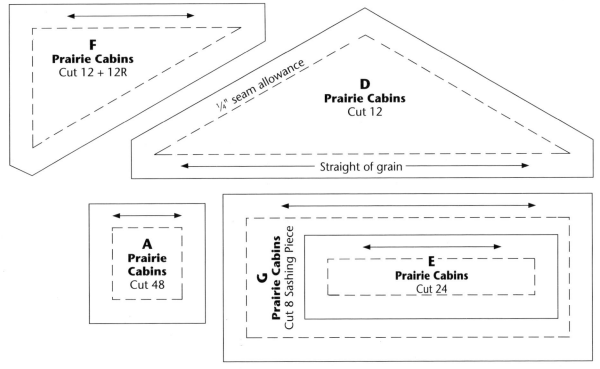

F
Prairie Cabins
Cut 12 + 12R

¼" seam allowance

D
Prairie Cabins
Cut 12

Straight of grain

A
Prairie Cabins
Cut 48

G
Prairie Cabins
Cut 8 Sashing Piece

E
Prairie Cabins
Cut 24

How in Tarnation Did Those Trees?...

by Mary Hickey

It was dawn in the high mountain country. Frosty dawn. I could hear the thump-thumping of Ben's feet racing across the hall floorboards, the whoosh as he scooped our clothes off the chair by the stove, and the thump-thump as he hurried back toward the bed. Just as he rounded the corner and started through our door, I lifted the quilts and he dove back under the covers. Grinning, he shoved my warm dress, socks, and sweaters over to me, while he started wiggling into his own woolen pants.

"Pa's eating the bacon and flapjacks she cooked. Do you think he likes it here? Do you think we'll get to stay, Emma?" Ben asked.

"I think he likes it, but I thought he liked it in Leadville and we didn't stay." I wanted to stay here, too. We had been at Mrs. Haller's warm boarding house for three weeks. Mrs. Haller was kind, and her daughter, Meg, was my friend.

"I like it here better than Leadville and Crested Butte and way better than Grandby. I hope we get to stay," mumbled Ben through the sweater he was yanking over his face.

Leadville, Crested Butte, Blue River, Tincup, Fairplay, Bonanza, and Frisco—those were the towns we had lived in since Ma had died of pneumonia two years ago in Grandby. This little town, Stonybrook, perched high above the tree line in the Rocky Mountains, was by far the best. Pa had a real job at the railroad station, the Hallers were gentle and generous, and we could go to school. It was cold here, but the sun shimmered on the frosty hillsides, and the stars were close enough to reach up and touch. I loved it here in Stonybrook.

"I don't know, Ben," I said, enjoying the last seconds of warmth before I jumped out of bed. "But if we don't get going, we're going to miss breakfast."

Ben popped out of bed and jammed his feet into his boots. "Maybe if I'm really good and quiet and do all my chores, we can stay."

"You'd never be able to be quiet, Ben, but I don't think that's why we keep moving."

"Then, why do we?" He looked so worried.

Ben was one year younger than me. But at nine, he was already bigger than me. His hair was light brown and his clear blue eyes were eager and curious. He found his school work easy and often rushed through it.

"I don't know. Pa says he misses trees here in Stonybrook, but I don't think that's it. I guess he's looking for something, but he doesn't know what it is."

We hurried down to the kitchen where Pa and the other boarders were pulling on coats before walking uphill toward the railroad office.

"Bye, Pa," said Ben, throwing his arms around Pa's big shoulders.

"Good-bye, Sprout. Bye, Emma," he said, kissing the top of my head.

We watched him walk to the road. He stood for a minute, gazing far across the steep hillsides toward the dark patches of forest. High in the mountains, the wind and cold last so long the trees cannot grow. We had never before lived without trees. Pa missed the wind whistling and whooshing through the needles of the Douglas fir and the light flickering on the branches of the western red cedar.

"Pretty soon, we'll move back to where there are some good trees," Pa would say, thinking he was reassuring us. Oh, Ben and I liked trees. Not as much as Pa did, but we liked trees. We just liked Stonybrook and the Hallers better. Also, we knew that when we moved to the place with trees, Pa would miss something else, and we would move on again.

"Emma," Ben said, his voice low, "can't we find some way to keep Pa here?"

I studied Ben's worried face.

"We'll get him to stay. I'm not sure how," I said, holding his hand. "But we'll get him to stay."

At the boarding house in Bonanza, Ben and I had not been allowed in the kitchen or parlor. We had to stay in our room all the time after school and in the evening. We even had to eat our meals in the room, sitting on a box. The landlady in Crested Butte sniffled constantly and wiped her nose on her apron. At the rooming house in Blue River, we had to share a room with Pa and three other miners who snored. In Tincup, the woman who owned the house made us scrub her pine floors from dawn to dusk to make up for the wear and tear we kids had on her house. The lady in Fairplay gave us only bitter coffee and a piece of greenish bread for breakfast.

Mrs. Haller liked us in the kitchen and gave us biscuits and jam after school. The smell of pies cooling on the drainboard and the sound of the sewing machine whirring greeted us in the afternoon.

"Emma, how would you like to make a little quilt like Meg's?" she asked that afternoon. She smelled comfortable— like soap and apples. "I have some green scraps left from my dress that you could have. And there are some good bits of muslin in the scrap bag."

I felt my heart jump with excitement. Meg worked on her pretty quilt every evening. I loved watching as the little scraps and snippets of fabric magically turned into twinkling stars. I knew instantly what I wanted to make.

"Oh, yes!" I could only breathe the words. "I'd like to make a quilt with trees on it."

"Well, I have a nice pattern for a pine tree. Let's get you started right now."

Ben wolfed down three biscuits and ran out to play on the hillside.

Mrs. Haller opened her envelope of saved paper. Taking out a stiff card, she traced and cut four triangles. Smiling, she showed me how to place the paper pattern on the fabric and draw around it with a pencil.

"It's good to be careful while you draw the shapes, Emma, but you don't have to hold your breath," she said, laughing.

"I'm afraid I'll break the pencil point, and I want it to be perfect," I said nervously.

"It will be perfect," she reassured me.

After I traced the shapes on the fabrics, Meg showed me how to cut them just inside the pencil line.

I hated to stop when Meg and Mrs. Haller started supper. I went outside to find Ben and help him load the wood box and carry water from the well.

Ben was digging a fort in the hillside.

"It's going to be as big as the train tunnel," he claimed. "I'm a really good digger like Pa," he said, his eyes wide with excitement. It was amazing how deep a hole he had dug in the cold ground. He was standing in the hole up to his waist.

"Do you think Mrs. Haller will mind you diggin' up her ground like that?" I wondered aloud.

Ben looked stricken.

"Will she be mad, Emma? I can fill it up. I'll bring a lantern and fill it right after supper if she's mad."

"No," I said thoughtfully. "No, Ben. Leave it alone. I'll ask her if you can dig a fort out here, and if she says 'No,' then you can fill it in."

I walked slowly over to the woodshed, planning. I just might have a use for that hole.

Mrs. Haller thought that digging a big hole was a "good way to use up that boy's extra energy," and I thought that the hole might just be the start of a plan to get Pa to stay in Stonybrook.

Ben gulped his stew while Pa and the other men talked about the fight in town that afternoon. On his way out of the Silver Nugget Saloon, a miner had bumped into an old settler named Ear-less Earl. He was called Ear-less because of some damage to his ear in a fight with a bear. He was a huge man with no neck, a lumpy face, matted gray hair, and a missing front tooth. The miner got mad at Ear-less and punched him.

"That Ear-less, he may be old, but he's as tough and strong as that old mule he rides. He just picked up that Gus and tossed him over the porch rail like he was a pesky beetle," Pa said.

"Yep. He may look old and crazy, and he's harmless till you cross him. Then, watch out!" Bill Craddock said.

"He's wonderful at finding berries," Meg whispered to me. "He takes us kids down to Putnam Hollow every summer so we can pick huckleberries and blackberries. Then, he hangs our buckets on Lucinda's back to carry them home for us."

"I wish I could go with you," I said.

"Of course, you can," Meg said. "All the kids in town go at least once. I go every day for weeks. Ma keeps jars and jars of berries in the cellar. That's why we can have so many pies all winter."

The talk drifted to other subjects.

"Are you going to the Literary Sunday, Mr. Allen?" Mrs. Haller asked, looking at Pa.

"No," Pa said slowly. "I thought I'd take Ben and Emma down to Putnam Hollow for the day to look at the town."

Ben looked at me with panic in his eyes. We both knew that Pa was thinking of moving again. I would have to work fast to keep us in Stonybrook.

Ben had a fight at school the next day. Moosie Everret socked Ben because he was a newcomer. Ben and Moosie tussled for about five minutes while the other boys stood in a ring and yelled. Ben blackened Moosie's eye and now they were best friends. Moosie came every afternoon to help Ben dig a new, bigger fort.

Ear-less Earl came to Mrs. Haller's that week to repair a leaking section of her roof. When we came home from school, Ear-less was kneeling on

the roof, banging some new shingles onto a leaky spot. He grinned as he pointed to Ben's growing fort.

"That's some hole yer diggin', boy," he wheezed. "Yer gonna hit Chiny soon. Yep, yer some digger. They're gonna have to put you to work on the railroad, diggin' snow off the tracks."

"Do you think so?" Ben asked. "I'm making a fort. Then, if we get attacked, Emma and I can hide in here. That is, if we don't move away," he added wistfully.

"What fer would you move away?" Ear-less asked.

"Our Pa misses trees up here in Stonybrook," I interrupted. "He wants to move us to a town with some trees."

"Trees! Who needs trees up here? The air is fresh and you kin look out across hundreds of miles of mountaintops. And at night, you can just about touch the stars with your little finger. Why, it's almost like livin' in the sky!"

"Yes," I answered, "but our pa thinks he wants to move to Putnam Hollow where there are more trees. I just wish there were some way to have trees here in Stonybrook, but Pa says they won't grow this high in the mountains."

"Nope," he said with nails in his mouth. "I reckon we don't get enough warm days for trees to grow. Mrs. VanSander tried plantin' some saplings. But they never grew to be any more than jist little wispy things in this here cold."

Ben took his shovel and began to throw dirt from deep in his fort onto the growing mound of diggings.

That night, before we went to sleep, I whispered my plan to Ben.

"But how could we get them up here?" he asked, his eyes wide.

"Maybe Ear-less Earl and Lucinda would help us," I said.

Every afternoon, while Ben and Moosie worked on the fort, I pieced the trees of my quilt. Mrs. Haller said I did a good job. I liked sewing the little shapes together. It helped me forget my anxiety about moving again. The trees were the pretty greens of Mrs. Haller's Sunday dress.

While I stitched, I thought about asking Ear-less Earl's help. But, what if he said no? Or worse, what if he laughed at us and told everyone in town? I didn't see him again that week to ask.

Sunday dawned sunny and cold. Mrs. Haller packed some sandwiches and apple muffins and tea in a basket for us to take. She didn't act like she knew that Pa was thinking about moving to Putnam Hollow, but she looked puzzled and sad when we drove out of the barn.

Pa was happy bumping along the trail. He let us each sit on his lap and drive the wagon for a while. Then, he taught us a new song called "Major McNamara's Mule." We had to sing each chorus faster and faster until all we could sing were the first two words before we started laughing too hard to sing.

When we got down to the forest, Pa stopped the wagon, and we all stood on the seat and broke off some low cedar branches. Tiny green buds were swelling on the tips of the limbs. Two skylarks chased each other through the treetops.

"Oh, just smell that good, clean cedar. And listen to the wind sing through that fir." Pa looked so happy that, just for a minute, I wanted to

move down near the trees, too.

The town of Putnam Hollow, like Stonybrook, stretched along a single steep road that sloped toward a tumbling creek. The mine there had a sign that said, "Closed, gone busted."

"Well, I guess it'd be pretty hard to find work here with the mine closed," Pa said.

Ben looked at me and smiled sadly. He wanted to stay in Stonybrook, but he wanted Pa to be happy, too.

We looked around a bit more, ate our lunch, and started back up the trail. The wind grew colder, so Ben and I sat in the back of the wagon. Pa piled hay around us and wrapped a quilt over our legs.

"Let's sing a warm song," he shouted above the wind. "In the great south seas, there lived a whale, and he could drink buckets of ginger ale . . ." We bellowed with him, laughing.

Ben was asleep when we pulled into the barn by Mrs. Haller's. She ran out and bundled me into the house, while Pa carried Ben in to bed. She had hot milk on the stove to warm us up. Pa looked at her a long time while she bustled around the kitchen.

"You're mighty nice to my young'uns," he said after a long time.

"Well, they're fine youngsters," she said, smiling.

"Not everyone has been so good to them," he said softly.

In the morning, when Ben dove back under the quilts with our warmed clothes, he said, "Pa has a sprig of cedar in his chest pocket and he's just staring out the window. She cooked his favorite breakfast, flapjacks, and he's not eating! Emma, do you think he's fixing to move again?"

I had to find a way to talk to Ear-less Earl. If we didn't do something soon, Pa would make up his mind and then it would be too late.

"Ben, I'm going to help you bring in the wood for the stove this morning. Let's hurry so we'll have time to eat some flapjacks."

We dressed quickly and raced to the wood-shed. I took Ben's arm and spoke to him earnestly.

"Ben, I'm going to move some logs from here to out behind the barn while you fill the wood box. That way, it will look like Mrs. Haller is getting low on firewood. Then, when we go in, I want you to tell her she's almost out."

He had to argue and ask questions, but I finally per-suaded him it was like playacting. He was pretty convincing when he told her.

"Oh, my gracious," she said. "I better talk to Ear-less Earl right away and have him haul some from near Ferndale Falls."

"If I see him, I'll tell him you're looking for him," I said sweetly. "Maybe, if he can do it Saturday, Ben and I can help him. We've never seen Ferndale Falls."

"All right, if you see him," she said, looking worried.

I felt guilty about upsetting her; she was so kind to us.

On the way home from school, we saw Lucinda munching outside the general store. We found Ear-less out back, repair-ing the back steps.

"I'll go down there and git it Saturday," he growled. His eyes were red and watery. "You kids better come along. You're the cause of her runnin' out so soon."

I couldn't sleep Friday night. I was so scared that Mrs. Haller and Ear-less would be angry when they found out all the fibs I'd been telling. And Pa, too. Pa never spanked us, but he could be real scary when he was angry.

Tiny blades of grass were poking through the ground, and a pale haze of green misted the tips of the huckleberry bushes on the trail down to Ferndale Falls. My stomach was tied in a hard little knot when we stopped for a drink of water.

"Er, Mr. Ear-less, Mrs. Haller isn't really out of wood," I said, trembling. "I lied because we need your help."

At first, he looked mad when I told him what we wanted to do. Then, he wrinkled up his nose and started to laugh. It started as a little "he-he" chuckle. Then, it grew to be a big laugh. Pretty soon, he was roaring with big wheezing "ha-has" and holding his sides. Then, Ben and I started to laugh. Then, Lucinda joined in with big "hee-haws." We all laughed so hard, we had to sit on the grass and wipe our eyes. I felt much better. All the way down the trail, Ear-less laughed in a puffing giggle.

Cutting down the trees was not nearly as hard as finding the right ones. They had to be perfect. One western red cedar and one Douglas fir. And tall. But, not too tall to drag behind Lucinda. Ben and I whacked at the fir while Ear-less chopped down the cedar. Then, he finished chopping down the fir. We lashed the bottoms of the trunks to the sides of Lucinda's pack saddle. That way, she could drag the tops of the trees behind her.

"Are the trees too heavy? Will they hurt her?" Ben worried.

"Nah. She'll jist think they're an ol' pair a toothpicks," Ear-less said, grinning. "You two will have to carry the axes and the canteen while I lead her. She won't work for nobody but me."

The sky turned all feathery pink as we started up the trail, and then the clouds turned lavender with silver-pink edges. Moonless dark covered the town by the time we neared the main street.

Piano music plinked from the saloon. We left the trees in the back while we went in and told Pa we were home. He was playing dominoes with Bill Craddock. We were too dirty to come into the kitchen, so we ate some stew and dumplings on the back steps with Ear-less.

After supper, Ear-less shoved the trunk of the cedar over to one of the holes. He roped the top of the tree to Lucinda and led her slowly uphill till the trunk slid into the hole and the tree stood upright. Ben and I shoveled dirt into the hole until the tree stood steady and tall. The Douglas fir was harder to stand straight. We got it up, but it leaned a little to the  west. Ear-less finally propped it up straight with a log.

Meg was the first to see the trees Sunday morning. She was surprised. Mrs. Haller was stunned. But Pa was stupefied.

"What in tarnation? Where the? . . . How on earth? . . ." he spluttered.

"Do you like them, Pa?" Ben asked.

Pa stared at Ben, at me, at the trees, and then at Ben and me again. "How did you? . . . Why on earth? . . ."

High up on the hill, a wheezing giggle drifted through the trees.

"Yes," said Pa softly. "Yes, I like them. These are the best trees in Colorado, right here in Stonybrook."

Strangers who visited Stonybrook that summer were always shocked at the sight of those two trees high above the timberline. A pair of skylarks nested in the cedar. Chipmunks moved in below the fir. And Mrs. Haller, Meg, and I sat and quilted on the porch swing in the shade of those two trees all summer.

Christmas that year, we burned the logs from the cedar, and I gave the little Tree quilt to Mrs. Haller. She gave it back to me when I left, ten years later, to teach school in Tincup.

Magic Trees

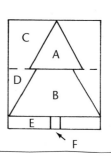

Quilt: 22½" x 26"
Block: 4" x 4½"
9 blocks

Materials: 44"-wide fabric

½ yd. green for outer border
¼ yd. assorted greens for trees and horizontal
  sashing
½ yd. light print for background in blocks and
  sashing
1 small scrap of red for tree trunks
¼ yd. stripe for inner border
¾ yd. backing fabric
Batting, binding, and thread

Cutting

All measurements include ¼"-wide seam allowances.
From the green border fabric, cut:
  2 strips, each 3" x 28", for side borders
  2 strips, each 3" x 25", for top and bottom borders
From the assorted greens, cut:
  3 strips, each 2" x 16½", for horizontal sashing
  9 Template A
  9 Template B
From the light print, cut:
  1 strip, 2" x 16½", for horizontal sashing
  9 + 9 Reversed Template C
  9 + 9 Reversed Template D
  18 Template E
  6 Template G
From the red, cut:
  9 Template F
From the stripe for inner border, cut:
  2 strips, each 1" x 22", for side borders
  2 strips, each 1" x 18", for top and bottom borders

Directions

1. Piece 9 blocks as shown.

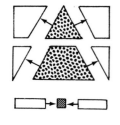

2. Sew blocks into rows of 3, with Template G pieces between the blocks as shown.

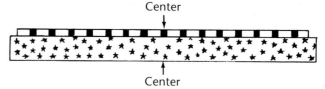

3. Stitch the rows together with green sashing strips.
4. Sew the light print strip to the top of the top row.
5. Center the inner border strips on the outer border strips and sew them together in pairs.

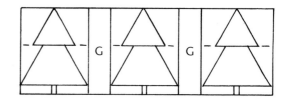

6. Sew the borders to the quilt top, mitering the corners. (See Mitered Corners, page 75.)
7. Layer with batting and backing.
8. Baste, quilt, and bind.

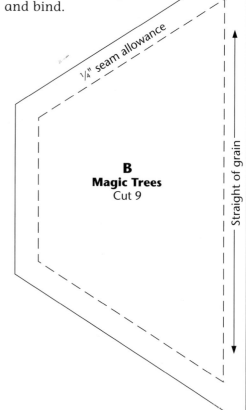

¼" seam allowance

Straight of grain

B
Magic Trees
Cut 9

Magic Trees by Mary Hickey, 1991, Seattle, Washington, 22½" x 26". A variety of green scraps grows into robust trees standing above strips of rocky grass. A narrow band of striped fabric in the border adds to the vigorous nature of this quilt. Quilted by Helen Hickey.

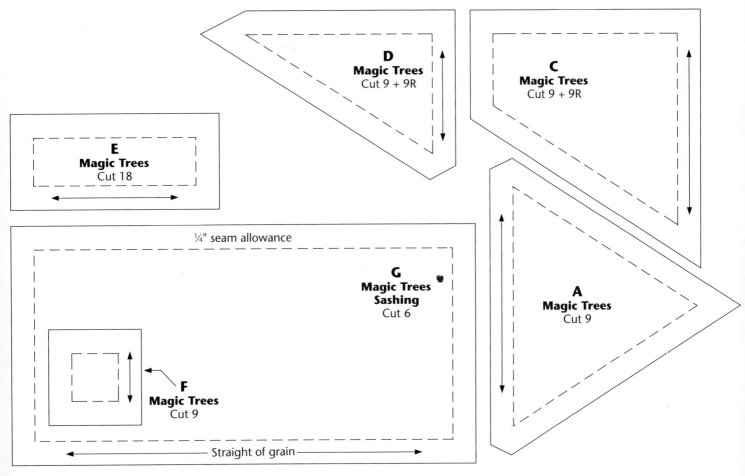

D
Magic Trees
Cut 9 + 9R

C
Magic Trees
Cut 9 + 9R

E
Magic Trees
Cut 18

¼" seam allowance

G
Magic Trees
Sashing
Cut 6

A
Magic Trees
Cut 9

F
Magic Trees
Cut 9

Straight of grain

Rocky Mountain Stars

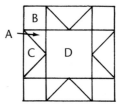

Quilt: 22½" x 29½"
Block: 5" x 5"
6 blocks

Materials: 44"-wide fabric

1 yd. striped floral fabric for outer border
⅛ yd. rose for inner border
¼ yd. assorted roses for stars
¼ yd. light print for background in blocks
¼ yd. black floral for star centers
¼ yd. rose for large set pieces
⅔ yd. backing fabric
Batting, binding, and thread

Cutting

All measurements include ¼"-wide seam allowances.
From the striped floral for outer border, cut:
    2 strips, each 4" x 32", for side borders
    2 strips, each 4" x 25", for top and bottom borders
From the rose for inner border, cut:
    2 strips, each 1" x 23", for side borders
    2 strips, each 1" x 16", for top and bottom borders
From the assorted roses for stars, cut:
    48 Template A
From the light print for background, cut:
    24 Template B
    24 Template C
From the black floral, cut:
    6 Template D
From the rose for set pieces, cut:
    2 Template X for large set squares (page 23)
    6 Template Y for side triangles (page 23)
    4 Template Z for corner triangles (page 23)

Directions

1. Piece 6 blocks as shown.

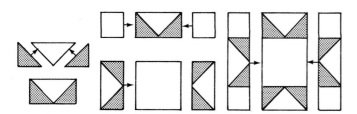

2. Sew the blocks in diagonal rows as shown.

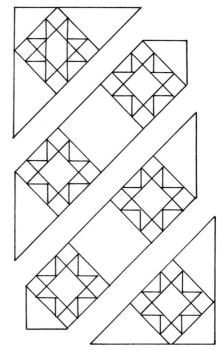

3. Stitch the rows together to form the quilt top.
4. Center the inner border strips on the outer border strips and sew them together in pairs.

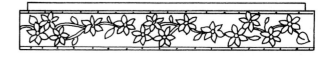

5. Stitch the borders to the quilt top, mitering the corners. (See Mitered Corners, page 75.)
6. Layer the quilt with batting and backing.
7. Baste, quilt, and bind.

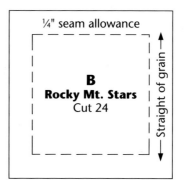

¼" seam allowance

B
Rocky Mt. Stars
Cut 24

Straight of grain

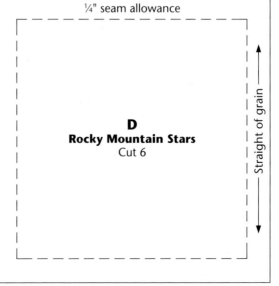

Rocky Mountain Stars by Mary Hickey, 1991, Seattle, Washington, 22½" x 29½". Bits of rose and black floral fabrics form striking stars. The quilt is finished with garlands of bouquets and ribbons reminiscent of the Victorian era.

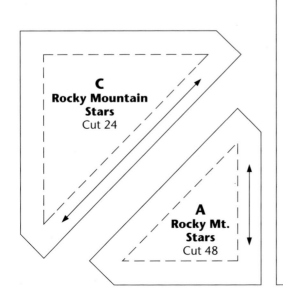

C
Rocky Mountain Stars
Cut 24

A
Rocky Mt. Stars
Cut 48

¼" seam allowance

D
Rocky Mountain Stars
Cut 6

Straight of grain

The Cottage at the Bottom of the Garden

by Kathleen Wagner

For as long as Johanna could remember, the old cottage at the bottom of the garden had been locked up tight as a wizard's secrets. The windows were frosted with dust. Ivy and brambly roses grew up the stone stairway and around the chimney and along the brick walls and almost as high as the roof peak. Pink columbine, blue forget-me-nots, white wind flowers, and red and purple foxglove poked up through the tall, ne-glected grass.

No one lived in the cottage anymore. In fact, for as long as Johanna could remember, no one had ever lived in the cottage. Her brothers called it "The Witch House" and told her tales of a queer, solitary woman who had lived there for many years. They described her fits of shrieking and the evil potions she brewed in the huge, rusted cauldron that still hung above the hearth.

"Her spirit still haunts these walls," Charles warned her, "since the day the townsfolk burned her at the stake." Nathaniel and John took up the chant.

"Grandpa says no witches were burned in Moody Corner," Johanna insisted, determined not to let them spoil her adventures, "only in Salem, more than a hundred miles away, and almost a hundred years ago in 1692. Ask him, if you don't believe me!"

The bottom of the garden was Johanna's special place, and if the truth were told, the tales her brothers wove only made the cottage that much more appealing.

The bottom of the garden was where Johanna went after the chickens, ducks, and geese had been fed, the eggs had been gathered, the bedding aired, the butter churned, the work shirts mended, the bread set to bake, and the soup to simmer. It was the place she ran to when her brothers, William, Henry, James, Charles, Nathaniel, and John teased her too much or ignored her too often or refused to let her play their games.

Johanna went to the bottom of the garden to watch the swallows dart and glide, to weave gillyflowers and coral bells and moonbeams into chains, to feed the briar rabbits, and to sit upon the creaky porch swing and rock Beth, the doll her grandmother had stitched for her, and to dream her favorite dreams.

She kept her treasures hidden there in a tin toffee box beneath the loose stone in the second step: a silver button shaped like a swan, an amber bead, three red parrot feathers, and a cowrie shell. All of them were gifts from her Uncle James, first mate on the Amphitrite, a great clipper ship that sailed the wide seas. He had returned to Boston Harbor loaded with books from England; coffee from Brazil; and tea, spices, and silks from as far away as India and China.

If only Johanna could sail with Uncle James and explore the wide, wonderful world, how happy she would be. But girls were not allowed to learn such occupations, and she would be forced to stay behind on Papa's farm when Charles went off in three weeks to serve as the Amphitrite's cabin boy, just as she'd been forced to stay at home when Henry rode off on their old gray cob to study law at Harvard College. The other brothers might escape as well—all except William, of course, who would stay behind to run the family farm when Papa grew too old to plow the fields and harvest the acres of hay and grain. But Johanna would have to stay behind to cook and clean and tend the poultry and the kitchen garden and stitch the linens and mend the work shirts until . . . until what? She asked her grandmother that question once, and the old woman had warned her that some day, some man, some William or Nathaniel or John, might come along, might choose her to cook his meals and clean his farmhouse and tend his poultry and his kitchen garden and stitch his linens and mend his work shirts and bear and raise his sons.

But Johanna was ten years old, and her grandmother's warnings were not to be considered. Someday, Johanna decided, she would leave her papa's farm and find a world of her own. In the meantime, though the cottage at the bottom of the garden was not India or China or even Boston, at least it was Johanna's own private place, and there she could spin her dreams.

She loved to go to the cottage when the sun was shining down on the daisies and the lavender and the larkspur. She loved it even more when the rain beaded up on the lady's mantle leaves and pattered gently on the porch roof and splashed in puddles on the ground.

She loved to walk down the windy, wooded path and come upon the little cottage, nestled in the cove like a cozy friend. Sometimes, she pretended she was an explorer discovering the cottage for the very first time.

There was only one more thing Johanna would have asked for. She wished she had a friend who loved the cottage as much as she did, a friend who liked to sing and liked to dream and liked to imagine thrilling adventures in exotic and faraway lands.

One gloomy day when the clouds hung low in the sky, Johanna made her way down the path,

and as she drew near the cottage, she heard a woman's voice singing softly nearby.

"Who could it be?" Johanna wondered. Not her mother, who was kneading bread dough in the big kitchen in the big house on the top of the rise. Not her grandmother, who sat knitting beside the wide kitchen hearth.

As Johanna moved closer, the singing grew louder. When she reached the clearing, she saw that the cottage door stood open and that smoke rose from the old stone chimney. Someone was inside the cottage—*her* cottage.

Johanna hid behind the trellis and peered through the dusty kitchen window at the woman inside. Her cloak was dark as night. On her head she wore a crimson shawl. She hummed a wordless tune and danced a curious waltz around the tiny kitchen. Her raised arms fluttered about her like the wings of a blackbird.

As the woman turned toward the window, she looked into Johanna's startled eyes. The little girl gasped, turned on her heels, and ran as fast as she could up the path toward home.

"Wait," the woman cried. "Don't go!" But Johanna, who had often imagined witches dancing in the glen, was too frightened when confronted by a real witch to stay.

"Mama! Mama!" she gasped as she burst through the kitchen door.

"Good grief, Johanna! What is it?" her mother demanded, splashing water from the large wooden bucket onto the stone floor. "Are you hurt, dear?"

"There's someone in the cottage, Mama. I think she's a witch!"

"Heavens, child! Is that what you're shrieking about? You gave me a such a fright, I've spilled the water. Fetch me some more as quick as you can or I won't be ready when your father and the boys come in for supper."

"But Mama, the witch . . . "

"I've no time for your foolish imaginings," her mother scolded, thrusting the bucket into her  hands and pushing her through the door toward the pump outside. "That's just Mary Blaine, your papa's cousin. She's come to live in the cottage."

It's my cottage, the girl wanted to say, but her mother would never have tolerated such a bold remark, so Johanna lifted the wooden handle and pumped. Her tears splashed silently into the big wooden bucket that slowly filled with water.

As the days and weeks dragged by, Mary Blaine made no move to vacate the cottage. She kept to herself, obviously happy with her own company, rarely visiting the big farmhouse, and then only late at night when Johanna was already in bed with Beth clasped snuggly in her arms.

"Mary Blaine's always been a queer one," Johanna's grandmother cautioned Johanna as they sat in the kitchen darning socks one morning. "Spent too much time alone when she was a girl, always spinning out queer stories. Next thing you know, she up and married that sea captain and shipped off with him to Zanzibar and Bora Bora and all those peculiar-sounding places

no Christian woman has any reason to see. If Jeremiah Blaine hadn't up and died of typhoid, she'd be out there still, sailin' the world, steerin' that ship of his, for all I know. No fit home. No proper family life. . . .

"You'd best be careful, Johanna. You don't stop livin' in that dream world of yours, you'll grow up to be just like her."

Would that be so bad? Johanna wondered as she spied on Mary Blaine from the path or from the branches of a tall, white oak that sent a shower of tiny acorns to the ground when she moved. Mary Blaine had traveled where she pleased, had seen faraway lands, and had had wonderful adventures.

And Mary Blaine was beautiful. Her hair was red and very long—almost the same color as Johanna's own hair. Sometimes, she wore it in braids down her back. Other times, it hung loosely to her waist, gleaming in the soft spring sunshine.

Mary Blaine wore loose-fitting gowns, white or beige or brown, and bright-colored shawls and paisley scarves. And when the morning air was icy cold, she wore the strange black cloak with the wide, winged sleeves.

Sometimes, Mary Blaine watched the swallows dart and glide, wove gillyflowers and coral bells and moonbeams into chains, fed the briar rabbits, and sat upon the creaky porch swing and dreamed her secret dreams.

Sometimes, she stitched tiny pieces of colored fabrics together into blocks, quilt blocks like the ladies made for Mama's quilting bees. But Mary Blaine's quilt blocks were like none Johanna had ever seen before. The colors—crimsons and azures and sapphires and magentas and purples and indigos—were as bright as the jewels in a Maharajah's crown. Johanna had seen the brilliant sheets of colored muslin drying on the line. And Mary Blaine's quilts, at least the two that Johanna had spied on the huge wooden quilting frames in the back room, were giant puzzles of intricate design, so vibrant they lit up the dim room with their colors.

But Mary Blaine was also a witch. Johanna's brothers had told her so, and she believed them, because sometimes Mary Blaine stayed inside the cottage for hours at a time, and then Johanna would smell strange, pungent odors escaping from inside. One day, Johanna worked up the nerve to tiptoe close to the cottage and peer in through the open window.

A wooden trunk stood open on the floor. Inside it, Johanna could see strange vials and jars of powders and murky liquids, bundles of twigs, roots, onion skins, and bark. Above the fire on the open hearth, the cauldron bubbled and boiled on the hob. Mary Blaine, in an apron and gloves, stirred the dark red liquid with a large wooden paddle, plunging deep into the bottom, and coming up with a large measure of fabric the color of blood. Johanna could hear her singing songs with the queer words that must be her magic spells. Droplets of the seething red liquid overflowed the huge pot, sputtering and hissing as they hit the dancing flames. The bitter odor floated through the window even stronger than before.

"Don't get too close," Johanna's brother John whispered, sneaking up behind her. "I saw her take some bugs out of that sea chest of hers, mash them into paste, and throw them in that soup she's boiling there. She's brewing a magic potion, and if she catches you spying on her, she'll make you drink it, and you'll turn into a big, black crow." He fled up the path, leaving Johanna, her heart banging frantically, to run home through the darkening woods alone. Mary Blaine had a sleek, black cat

she called Cassandra, who appeared and disappeared when Johanna least expected her, leaping from a tree branch or scurrying from behind the rose trellis.

"No one can hide from a witch's black cat," John warned her. "She'll spy on you just like you're spying on the witch, and then she'll slink back to tell her mistress, and the next thing you know, Farmer Hastings will be setting up his scarecrow to keep you out of his cornfields. I'd stay away from that witch if I were you—unless maybe you want to be just like her. Come to think of it, with that tangle of red hair and those green eyes of yours, you look kind of like her.

"I wonder what it feels like to be burned at the stake or hanged by the neck or tied to a chair and thrown into the river to drown?" he cackled as he walked away.

What if all the things John said were true? What if Cassandra really did spy on Johanna and carry tales back to the witch? Johanna didn't want to be an ugly, black crow, and she certainly didn't want to be a witch. At least, she didn't think she wanted to be a witch. She just wanted her treasures back—*her* treasures and *her* cottage. She couldn't stay away. Mary Blaine had stolen Johanna's special place, and her treasures were still hidden behind the loose rock in the second stone step. Johanna was determined to get them back, but while Mary Blaine stitched on her quilts in the back room, Cassandra kept watch on the porch or on the windowsill or in the doorway.

She watched and waited for her chance to sneak through the gate and onto the porch, but days went by and Mary Blaine almost never went away from the bottom of the garden. Those few times that she did, she left Cassandra to guard the cottage.

But then one day, Johanna saw Mary Blaine walk down the road to the village, carrying a marketing basket. Johanna crept close to the cottage, and for once, she could see no sign of Cassandra. This is my chance, she thought, and she scurried down the path and through the gate. She pushed the loose stone away and peered into the deep gap, but her toffee tin was gone! The witch had taken it! The witch had taken almost everything that Johanna loved.

Johanna rambled through the woods, kicking trees and plotting her revenge. I'll trample all the flowers at the bottom of the garden, she thought. I'll break all the cottage windows. I'll smash the old porch swing. But she couldn't bring herself to destroy the things she loved so much.

Johanna was still trying to think of a plan to get even with the red-haired witch, when, from the marshy quagmire down beside the stream, she heard a mournful shriek. She hurried to see what the noise was and found Cassandra trapped in a huge patch of briars. The more the cat struggled to pull away, the more the stickers bit into her smooth, black coat and the skin beneath.

"That'll teach you, you nasty spy," Johanna said. "You can stay there forever for all I care." She turned and walked away, but Cassandra's wailing followed her through the woods. Johanna ignored the cat's cries for as long as she could, but no matter how angry or frightened she was, she couldn't bear to think of the animal's fear.

"You may be a witch's cat," she said as she ripped at the tangled vines, "but I guess it's not your fault." Finally, she managed to set Cassandra free, but the cat's back leg was torn

and bleeding. Taking the blue ribbon from her long, red hair, Johanna bandaged the wound and carried the cat back to the cottage, laying her gently on the swing.

"Mary Blaine wants to see you," her mother told Johanna that night as she was laying the table for supper.

"You're to go to the cottage tomorrow at noon when you've finished your chores."

"But, Mama. . ."

"At noon," her mother repeated.

"Now you've had it," John whispered as they climbed the stairs to their beds in the loft. "She'll change you to a crow for sure."

Johanna dawdled on the path as long as she could, but soon she was at the front gate. It creaked and groaned as she pushed it. She forced her feet to carry her down the walk and up the stone stairs.

The front door was wide open. Johanna peeked inside. She didn't see Mary Blaine, but Cassandra lounged peacefully in the rocking chair. The cat meowed contentedly when she saw Johanna, then closed her eyes and went back to sleep.

The cottage smelled of cinnamon and apples. The table was set with rose-patterned china, sparkling silver, and crystal glasses. A jug of cosmos and baby's breath sat in the center. The room looked so inviting, Johanna almost forgot to be frightened.

If this were my cottage, she thought, it would look just like this.

Should I knock, she wondered, or ring the shiny brass bells that hung from the door? Before she could decide, Mary Blaine entered the kitchen from the back room.

"Come in, Johanna," she said. "I've been waiting for you."

Johanna swallowed hard and took one tentative step inside.

"I have something that belongs to you," the woman said, her voice sweet as music. She took Johanna's toffee tin down from the mantel and handed it to Johanna. Her belongings and her blue hair ribbon, washed now and rolled into a loop, were safe inside.

"And I have something else I think you might like," she added. She handed her a small bundle, wrapped in soft, blue fabric and tied with a deep-red ribbon. When Johanna opened it, she found a small, square quilt, just the right size for Beth, that was pieced with all the rainbow colors in the garden. Only a witch could have made such a quilt—a witch or a fairy.

"When I was just about your age," Mary Blaine told her as they ate bird's nest pudding and sipped chamomile tea, "I spent one summer playing outside this cottage. I hid my special

treasures in the gap in the stairs, and I made daisy chains and watched the swallows swoop and dive across the yard. I used to dream about the day I'd come back here to live, and now my dream's come true.

"But, now that my dream's come true, there's still one more thing I need. Can you guess what it is?"

Johanna shook her head.

"I need a friend to come and visit, to drink tea with me, and putter in the garden. A friend who will help me dye my fabrics and make my quilts; but most of all, a friend who loves the cottage as much as I do and isn't frightened by silly stories about witches. Do you know anyone like that?"

"I do," Johanna whispered. "I do."

Cozy Cats

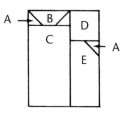

Quilt: 26" x 26"
Block: 3¼" x 4"
12 blocks
Templates: page 51

Materials: 44"-wide fabric

½ yd. light print for background and sashing
¼ yd. blue for cats and inner border
½ yd. lavendar floral for cats and outer border
⅛ yd. blue floral for cats
⅛ yd. lavender for cats
⅛ yd. pastel print for horizontal sashing
¾ yd. backing fabric
Batting, binding, and thread

Cutting

All measurements include ¼"-wide seam allowances.

Note: In her book, *Connecting Up*, Mary Ellen Hopkins shared a method for sewing tiny triangle corners to larger rectangles. To try this helpful method, cut Template A as a square and Templates B and E as rectangles. Dotted lines have been added to the templates to make this easier for you. The directions below will explain how to sew the pieces.

From the light background print, cut:
   12 Template A
   12 Template B
   12 Template D
   6 Template F
   1 strip, 2" x 16½", for the top piece of horizontal sashing
   2 strips, each 1½" x 18½", for side sashing
From the blue for cats and inner border, cut:
   6 Template A
   2 + 1R Template E
   3 Template C
   2 strips, each 1¼" x 18½", for inner border (sides)
   2 strips, each 1¼" x 20", for inner border (top and bottom)
From the lavendar floral for cats and outer border, cut:
   6 Template A
   1 + 2R Template E
   3 Template C
   2 strips, each 3½" x 20", for side borders
   2 strips, each 3½" x 26", for top and bottom borders
From the blue floral, cut:
   6 Template A

2 + 1R Template E
3 Template C
From the lavender, cut:
   6 Template A
   3 Template E
   3 Template C
From the pastel print, cut:
   3 strips, each 2" x 16½", for horizontal sashing

Directions

Note: Eight of the cats are facing left and four are facing right. Cats are very independent, so you will have to decide which way you want yours to face. Simply sew a Template A triangle to the right or left of Template E. I find it easier to sew the triangles for the ears (Templates A and B) and the back of the cat (Templates A and E) as connector squares.

1. Place 2 squares (Template A) against the background rectangle (Template B), right sides together, and 1 square (Template A) against the cat-back rectangle (Template E). Sew across the square diagonally from corner to corner.

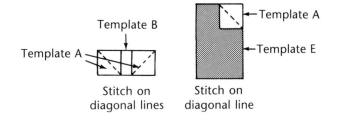

Template B
Template A
Stitch on diagonal lines

Template A
Template E
Stitch on diagonal line

2. Trim off the outside corner of the connector. Do not cut the corner off the background rectangle.
3. Fold the corner square back over the seam and press.

Fold and press;
do not trim

Fold and press;
do not trim

4. Piece 12 blocks as shown.

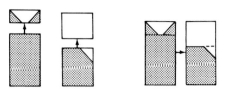

5. Take some time to arrange your cats in a pleasing composition. Sew the blocks together in rows of 4 as shown, using Template F pieces between the cats.

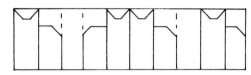

6. Sew a floral sashing strip to the bottom of each row.
7. Sew a background sashing strip to the top of the top row.
8. Sew the rows together to form the quilt top.
9. Stitch the side sashing strips to the sides of the quilt top.
10. Sew inner borders to the quilt, sides first, then the top and bottom.
11. Sew outer borders to the quilt, sides first, then the top and bottom.
12. Sew the outer borders to the top and bottom of the quilt.
13. Layer the quilt with batting and backing.
14. Baste, quilt, and bind.

Cozy Cats by Mary Hickey, 1991, Seattle, Washington, 26" x 26". Engaging cats snuggle together and stand aloof in this periwinkle and purple quilt. From the collection of Kathleen and Stan Wagner.

Puss in the Corner

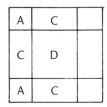

Quilt: 27½" x 27½"
Block 4" x 4"
25 blocks (13 Block I, 12 Block II)

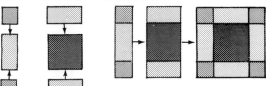

Materials: 44"-wide fabric

½ yd. cream fabric for Block II
⅛ yd. cream floral for small squares
¼ yd. pink for rectangles
¼ yd. red print for large squares
⅛ yd. inner border fabric
½ yd. outer border fabric
⅞ yd. backing fabric
Batting, binding, and thread

Cutting

All measurements include ¼"-wide seam allowances.
From the cream fabric, cut:
    12 Template B (for Block II)
From the cream floral, cut:
    52 Template A
From the pink fabric, cut:
    52 Template C
From the red print, cut:
    13 Template D
From the inner border fabric, cut:
    2 strips, each 1½" x 20½", for side
        borders
    2 strips, each 1½" x 22½", for top
        and bottom borders
From the outer border fabric, cut:
    2 strips, each 3" x 22½", for side
        borders
    2 strips, each 3" x 27½", for top
        and bottom borders

Directions

1. Piece 13 Block I as shown.

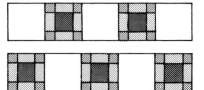

2. Sew Blocks I and II together in rows as shown.

3. Sew the rows together to form the quilt top.
4. Stitch inner borders to the quilt, sides first, then the top and bottom.
5. Sew the outer borders to the quilt, sides first, then the top and bottom.
6. Layer with batting and backing.
7. Baste, quilt, and bind.

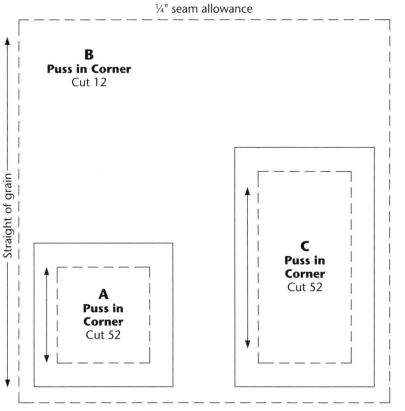

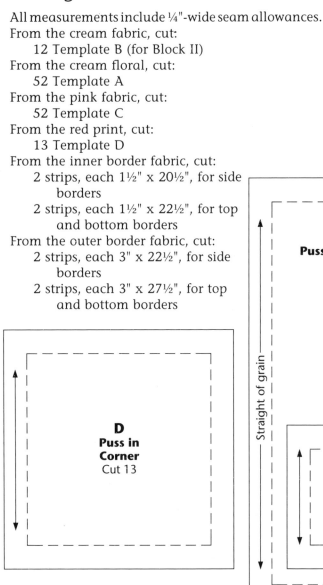

Puss in the Corner by Peg Storey, 1991, Seattle, Washington, 27½" x 27½". Peg used striking red bouquets as the focal point of the blocks. Smaller sprigs of flowers fill the corners, and coral pink finishes the sides of these endearing blocks. Chintz fabric was greatly prized in the eighteenth century and appears here in the set blocks and border.

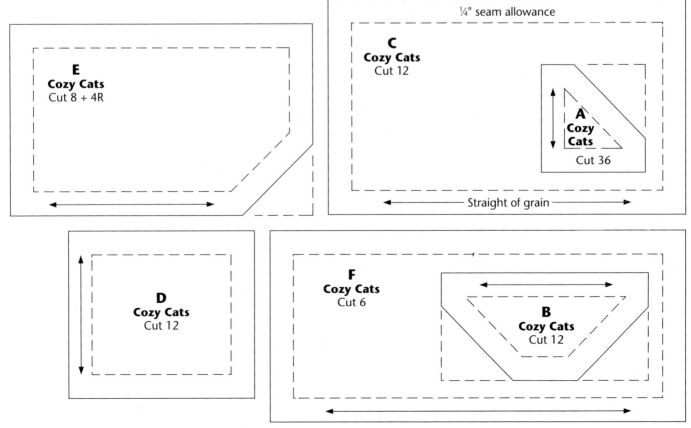

E
Cozy Cats
Cut 8 + 4R

¼" seam allowance

C
Cozy Cats
Cut 12

A
Cozy Cats
Cut 36

Straight of grain

D
Cozy Cats
Cut 12

F
Cozy Cats
Cut 6

B
Cozy Cats
Cut 12

Sailing Ships

Quilt: 22" x 25¾"
Block: 3½" x 4¾"
9 blocks

Materials: 44"-wide fabric

½ yd. blue fabric for background in blocks and sashing
½ yd. assorted red fabrics for boats and border
⅛ yd. white print for sails
¾ yd. backing fabric
Batting, binding, and thread

Cutting

All measurements include ¼"-wide seam allowances.
From the blue fabric, cut:
    4 strips, each 2" x 17", for horizontal sashing
    9 Template A
    9 Template B
    18 Template C
    9 Template D
    18 Template E
    12 Template G for sashing between the blocks
From the red fabrics, cut:
    2 strips, each 3" x 28", for side borders
    2 strips, each 3" x 24", for top and bottom borders
    9 Template F
From the white print, cut:
    9 Template A
    9 Template B

Directions

1. Piece 9 blocks as shown.

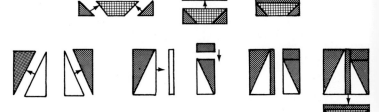

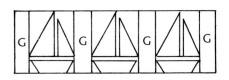

2. Sew the blocks into rows of 3 as shown.

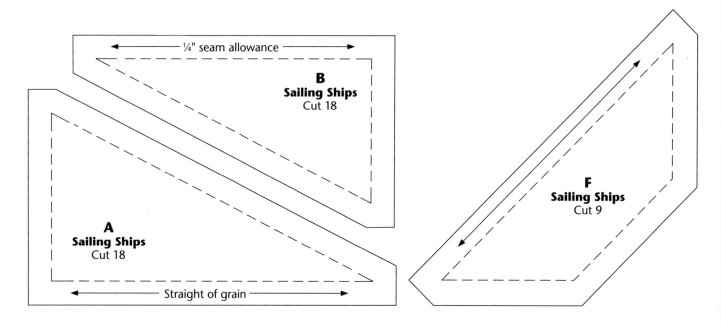

3. Stitch the rows together with the sashing strips to form the quilt top.
4. Stitch the borders to the quilt top, mitering the corners. (See Mitered Corners, page 75.)
5. Layer with batting and backing.
6. Baste, quilt, and bind.

¼" seam allowance

B
Sailing Ships
Cut 18

A
Sailing Ships
Cut 18

Straight of grain

F
Sailing Ships
Cut 9

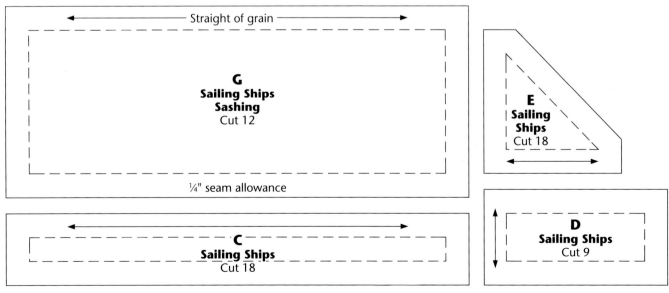

Sailing Ships by Mary Hickey, 1990, Seattle, Washington, 22" x 25¾". Sailboats and ships were a favorite theme in pioneer quilts. Jaunty ships ride a cobalt sea in this modest little quilt.

← Straight of grain →

G
Sailing Ships
Sashing
Cut 12

¼" seam allowance

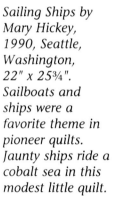

E
Sailing Ships
Cut 18

C
Sailing Ships
Cut 18

D
Sailing Ships
Cut 9

Granny's Puckered Puzzle

by Mary Hickey

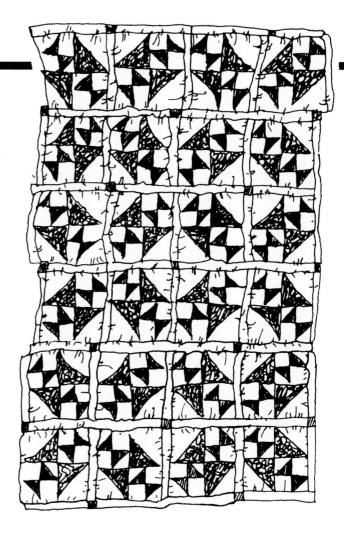

Anna's brown hair grew damp against her temples as she twisted and fidgeted in her chair. Her cousins, Alecia and Sara, ladylike in their Sunday dresses, quietly embroidered their samplers. Anna felt clumsy and inept next to her dainty cousins. She was trying to stitch a tiny violet, intertwined with the letter "E," onto a fine linen handkerchief. It was to be a present for her grandmother's sixtieth birthday. She had stitched and unstitched the tiny flower so many times that a pale lavender stain had started to form on the exhausted linen fabric.

Beads of perspiration stung the back of her neck and pricked her waist. How could she ever endure sewing like this for the rest of the beautiful afternoon? The sun was still high in the enormous, curved sky. Shadows from the wispy clouds waltzed over the endless prairie grasses, weaving and waving in the wind. The sheep, the cows, the horses, even the oxen called now and again, inviting Anna outdoors to visit them.

The inside of the cabin was still new, and the smell of pine shavings was comforting. A fat beetle waddled across the windowsill. Anna's eyes drifted to the big

stove at the far end of the room. She loved the curved legs and the pretty clusters of grapes embossed on the heavy iron doors. Anna thought of Granny wearing her dark purple dress and sitting near her stove in Sioux Falls. Granny's blue eyes curved into twinkling crescents when she smiled, and her wispy gray hair constantly escaped the little bun on the top of her head.

"Anna, just twist the thread twice around the needle for the French knots," Aunt Charlotte said.

"So many twists will make too big a knot."

Flustered, Anna looked at the lumpy knot forming on the handkerchief and bent her head over her work. Her soft brown braids parted at her neck and tumbled forward over her shoulders. Oh, would she ever learn to like sitting so still and doing such tiny, painstaking work? The lovely Sunday afternoon crept along. Her shoulders and the back of her neck began to ache. Her legs were cramped and her fingers cried out to hold Blackie's reins and fly across the prairie on his broad back. She dared not peek out the window again. Aunt Charlotte seemed to notice everything she did. She scrunched down smaller in her chair and started again on the sprinkle of French knots that would complete the handkerchief.

"When you finish the handkerchief, I'll help you wash and press it. Then you can wrap it in the tissue we've been saving for Grandmother's presents," Aunt Charlotte said, smiling.

"Will you be able to finish the quilt for Granny before her birthday?" Alecia asked.

"I have all but ten of the blocks pieced, but it will take several weeks to sew the blocks into the quilt top. I was hoping to have a quilting bee the Saturday after school starts in September, but I don't suppose I can sew up the whole top in less than two weeks," Aunt Charlotte sighed.

"Maybe we could help," Sara suggested. Anna felt her heart leap. She loved the sparkling red and green triangles dancing on the quilt blocks. She would not mind sitting still if she could sew a quilt block for Granny.

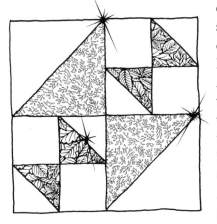

"No, we have to make over the hand-me-down dresses that Aunt Minnie sent from Iowa. You girls will need new dresses for the fall session of school and for Granny's birthday," said Charlotte.

Hand sewing consumed endless hours on the homestead. The making and remaking of shirts, trousers, dresses, and linens had to be done along with cooking, cleaning, laundering, and gardening. To supplement the family income, Aunt Charlotte also made shirts for some bachelor homesteaders in the area. But when Aunt Charlotte worked on her quilt, her face softened with pleasure.

"Oh, I love the blue dress Aunt Minnie sent!" Sara said. Her voice bubbled with joy at the thought of the rare new dress.

"I thought I'd make yours from the blue print, Sara, and the green and rose can be yours, Alecia, but I don't know what would look best on you, Anna. Maybe the red calico would set off your brown hair." Charlotte said. She smiled kindly at Anna.

Anna felt her cheeks turn scarlet as her blonde cousins considered her. Anna's eyes had feasted on the lovely dresses in Aunt

Minnie's box. She had liked the red dress with its black trim, inset lace, and wide, cream-colored collar. But now, shyness choked her from answering.

"I think you would look pretty in the red dress, Anna," Alecia said kindly.

Anna nodded dumbly and tried to smile.

"Anna, you still have one more leaf to chain stitch. See here, next to the top of the E." Aunt Charlotte pointed to the faint, gray outline on the crumpled linen.

Anna knew Aunt Charlotte tried to be kind, indeed, she was kind in a distant way. But kindness alone would not weave Anna into the fabric of this family. She had heard terrible stories about orphans forced to do almost slave labor for their keep. Anna knew she was fortunate to have an Aunt Charlotte and an Uncle Edmund who would take her in and treat her with such gentleness. She did not mind the hard work. Everyone in the new Dakota territories toiled, and Aunt Charlotte was fair in what she asked. Anna enjoyed milking, feeding, herding, weeding, washing, churning, and sweeping.

It was the sitting-still and being-a-lady kind of work that made her eyes blur with tears for her old life—the life before typhoid fever stole her mother and father away—the homestead life so similar to this, and yet so different, because she had belonged in her own little family and was treasured by her gentle mother and sturdy father. What Anna could not understand was that it was the gulf of pain and loss in her heart that created her sense of distance from Aunt Charlotte. And it was on Sundays, when only quiet handwork could be done, that Anna felt the great emptiness that washed over her now.

When she had completed three French knots, Anna stole a glance at the sparkling sky. A meadowlark swooped and dove in the wind. Still two hours of sitting left. As she lowered her eyes to her needle, she thought she saw a speck on the horizon. Maybe Uncle Edmund and Eddie were returning from their long trip to Sioux Falls.

Anna forced her eyes back to her sewing. Aunt Charlotte was working on her puzzle quilt. Anna loved watching the triangles become little squares and the little squares become rows and the rows become blocks as Aunt Charlotte's deft fingers made the needle fly through the fabrics. Anna felt that if she could sew a quilt, she would not mind the quiet work of Sundays. But every time she thought of asking Aunt Charlotte, a lump of shyness welled up in her throat and the words became tangled on her tongue.

Anna pretended to sneeze and glanced out the window. The speck was now a dot rolling slowly closer. Sara noticed the dot, too.

"It's Papa! I think it's Papa coming!"

Shading their eyes, they went to the porch and squinted at the tiny silhouette advancing toward them.

"It is Papa!" Alecia squealed. They all rushed toward the rumbling wagon.

Uncle Edmund was as big and loud as Aunt Charlotte was dainty and soft-spoken. Mamma used to say that Uncle Edmund was born in a roaring storm and had spent his life living up to it. Mamma had always been surprised and pleased that her big, boisterous brother had married such a fine, quiet

woman as Charlotte. While Anna was afraid of him, she also felt safe with him.

Today, as he reined in Blackie and Buttercup, he was a one-man riot, shouting orders to Eddie; bear hugging everyone, including Anna; stomping around the spring wagon; throwing boxes, crates, and sacks to the ground. Then, with one last roar, he presented Aunt Charlotte with an enormous wooden crate.

"I got this with the money from that mean heifer we sold. It should make you a whirling whiz of a sewer, Charlotte," Uncle Edmund bellowed in his good-natured way.

Anna watched as Uncle Edmund and Eddie set the crate in the dusty grass and pulled the boards apart. There in the box was a large machine—a machine for sewing.

Anna stared in awe at the magical machine. Its long needle and nickel parts sparkled and its varnished wood glowed. On a thin, black ridge stood a spool of thread. By whirling the wheel with one hand, Aunt Charlotte could start it. Then, working the treadle with her feet, she could keep the needle whirring up and down. Anna felt dizzy as she watched the needle wink through the little hole in the nickel plate.

"Edmund, this was far too costly. You should have saved that money for a corn planter," Aunt Charlotte said. "We can't possibly afford such an expensive machine."

"Nonsense!" Uncle Edmund roared, grinning. "With the machine to help with the sewing, maybe you can spare me one of the girls to herd the cows."

"If you need help with the cows,

one of the girls can do it whether we have this machine or not. You really should not have spent so much money on a machine just for sewing."

Anna smiled as she listened to Aunt Charlotte fuss. Anyone could see she was thrilled. Anna stroked the little brass oval on the front of the machine. It read "Isaac Merrit Singer, 1868."

During the last scorching week of August, Anna helped on the homestead. She gazed with pleasure at the wild foxglove blooming in graceful sweeps on the prairie. Briar roses and wild violets scented the winds as she milked the cow and churned butter. While she hoed in the garden, great white puffs of clouds sailed in the sky. In the late afternoons, while supper was bubbling on the stove, she and Sara and Alecia worked on their embroidery and Aunt Charlotte cut and remade the hand-me-down dresses on her new sewing machine. Sometimes, Alecia would work at the machine while Aunt Charlotte worked on her puzzle quilt blocks.

"Sixty-five, sixty-six, sixty-seven," Aunt Charlotte counted. "Only five more to make. I do so hope I can finish this quilt in time for your grandmother's birthday."

"Now that we have the sewing machine, you'll be able to, won't you, Mamma?" Alecia asked.

"Well, since I made the other blocks by hand, I'll have to sew the last few by hand, too, so they will all be the same," Charlotte said.

"Can you sew them to each other on the new machine?" Sara asked.

Anna glanced over at the wonderful, shiny machine. She loved guiding the straight side seams of shirts under the dancing needle.

"I think I can sew the blocks into the quilt top on the machine. The ladies from the nearby homesteads are coming in two weeks to quilt it with us," Charlotte said.

With all the work there was to do on the homestead, the progress on the quilt was slow.

Anna tried to do extra chores so Charlotte could finish the blocks. At last, on a windy day in early September, Anna watched as Aunt Charlotte hand stitched the last seam of the last block.

Anna, Sara, and Alecia cleared a space on the scrubbed floor and spread out the quilt blocks. They climbed the ladder to the loft and looked over the rail at the blocks on the floor below. Anna thought she had never in her life seen anything so beautiful. The tiny red, green, and gold triangles danced and sparkled in the little cabin. As Anna stared, the triangles grouped to form squares, but when she blinked, they split into stars. What a glorious gift it would be for their darling Granny!

Charlotte sat right down and started to sew the blocks to each other on the sewing machine while the girls prepared supper. When Uncle Edmund and Eddie came in from the wheat field for supper, they brought Mr. Wilcox, who had just returned from Sioux Falls.

"How do, Charlotte. I just come to bring you word that your sister, Adelia, scalded her arm putting up green beans. It looks like she could use a hand with that baby and those three little fellers of hers," Mr. Wilcox said.

"Gracious! Yes, of course, I'll go. These girls are plenty big enough to take care of the chores around here. My goodness, yes, but how will I ever get to Sioux Falls?"

"Jack says the Campbells are going to start out for Sioux Falls in the morning. You can probably ride with them," said Uncle Edmund, for once sounding subdued.

"Yep. I can stop by Campbells on my way

home and tell them to come by for you," Mr. Wilcox said.

"Then it's settled," Aunt Charlotte announced, bustling about as she gathered her bag and clothes to take to Sioux Falls.

Throughout that evening and well into the night, Anna could hear the rackety hum of the sewing machine as Charlotte worked to finish the quilt before she left for Sioux Falls. Anna awoke in the morning, expecting to see the gorgeous quilt, but it was folded up in Aunt Charlotte's sewing basket with a clean towel over it.

Anna hugged Aunt Charlotte good-bye and watched her step briskly onto Campbell's wagon. Observing her strained face as the wagon swung out onto the lane, Anna knew that Aunt Charlotte was disturbed about Adelia but sensed that there was something more.

After lunch, Anna lifted the towel from Charlotte's sewing basket and unfolded the quilt. She could see now what had caused the added distress on her aunt's face. Something had gone wrong with the tension of the sewing machine. In the poor light of the oil lamp, Charlotte had not realized that the blocks were puckering and gathering as they were being sewn into rows. As Anna studied the puckered and bumpy quilt, she realized Aunt Charlotte would never be able to take it apart and restitch it before Granny's birthday.

Anna understood how much Aunt Charlotte had wanted to finish the quilt for Granny's birthday. She knew that it would not be ready for the quilting bee and that Aunt Charlotte would be unable to give it to Granny to warm her old knees in the coming winter.

Anna sensed that creating the quilt made it

possible for Aunt Charlotte to endure the bone-grinding work of the homestead. That night, when the rest of the family had fallen into an exhausted sleep, Anna slipped out of bed and crept down the ladder from the loft. She took a candle stub from the box behind the stove and the tiny, sharp scissors from the sewing basket. Sitting on the porch, she started to snip apart the blocks.

With her slender shoulders hunched over in the dim light, she snipped and picked at the puckered seams. The ripping was slow, tedious, sitting-down, being-a-lady kind of work. Painstak-ingly, she picked apart the blocks. As Anna plucked at the thousands of stitches, she began to wonder how Aunt Charlotte was doing in Sioux Falls. She wondered if Charlotte could see the same moon that was rising in the starry sky over the whispering prairie, if she had picked some of the black raspberries that grew along the wagon road, and if she had seen the grasshoppers bouncing through the wild daisies near Sioux Falls. Anna thought of Granny's gentle smile and of her busy hands, always sewing or knitting. Night after night that week, she picked and plucked at the endless stitches in the faint light until she could no longer hold her eyelids up. But during the daytime, she felt a curious warmth.

Late Friday night, her hands trembled with excitement as she ripped apart the last blocks.

Saturday evening, Aunt Charlotte returned home.

"Oh, I am so glad to be back. Aunt Adelia is going to be fine. Oh, I missed you all so much!" Charlotte exclaimed, stepping down from Campbells' wagon. "I am just so glad to be home. Sioux Falls is so crowded and noisy and dusty! And I missed my girls!"

Alecia and Sara crowded close to Charlotte as she bustled toward the house. Aunt Charlotte hugged each of them and then reached out to Anna. Anna held her breath as Aunt Charlotte softly stroked her cheek and smoothed her hair.

"Anna, I missed you very much," she whispered as she gently embraced her. Charlotte smelled of lavender and fresh air. Anna snuggled close to her and felt warm and safe.

"I have something to show you, Aunt Charlotte," Anna murmured into Aunt Charlotte's ear.

Great tears rolled down Aunt Charlotte's face when she saw the blocks all separated.

"Oh, Anna! I wanted so much to finish Granny's quilt for her birthday. And now I'll be able to," she cried.

Sunday afternoon, while Charlotte finished her quilt, Anna started one. Beginning her first quilt made the sitting still bearable, even pleasant, as she stitched the little squares of her Swallow's Nest blocks. And slowly, Anna came to realize that in ripping apart the blocks for Aunt Charlotte, she had allowed herself to be pieced into this new family.

Granny's Puzzle

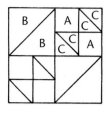

Quilt: 24" x 33"
Block: 4" x 4"
24 blocks

Materials: 44"-wide fabric

⅜ yd. green for border
¼ yd. assorted greens for triangles
1 yd. for background in blocks
¼ yd. fabric for sashing (Notice that the quilt in the photograph uses the same fabric for background and for sashing.)
¼ yd. assorted reds for triangles and set squares
¾ yd. backing fabric
Batting, binding, and thread

Cutting

All measurements include ¼"-wide seam allowances.
From green for border, cut:
    2 strips, each 3" x 26", for top and bottom borders
    2 strips, each 3" x 35", for side borders
From assorted greens, cut:
    96 Template C
From background fabric, cut:
    96 Template A
    48 Template B
    96 Template C
    26 Template D (sashing pieces)
    14 Template F (sashing pieces)
    4 Template G (sashing pieces for outer corners)
From assorted reds, cut:
    48 Template B
    17 Template E (set pieces)

Directions

1. Sew 24 blocks as shown.

2. Sew blocks together in rows of 4 as shown, adding a Template D piece between each block.

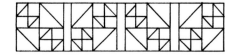

3. Stitch 2 rows of sashing and set pieces as shown.

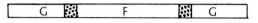

4. Stitch 2 rows of sashing and set pieces as shown.

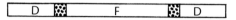

5. Stitch 3 rows of sashing and set pieces as shown.

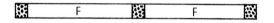

6. Sew the rows together with the sashings to form the quilt top.
7. Sew the borders to the quilt top, mitering the corners. (See Mitered Corners, page 75.)
8. Layer with batting and backing.
9. Baste, quilt, and bind.

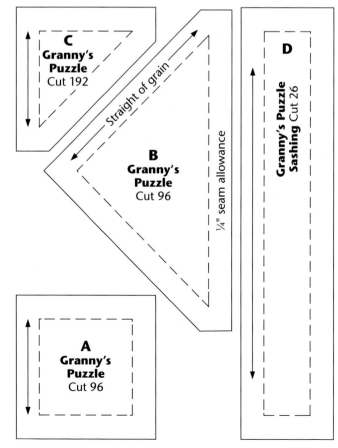

C
Granny's Puzzle
Cut 192

Straight of grain

B
Granny's Puzzle
Cut 96

¼" seam allowance

D
Granny's Puzzle Sashing Cut 26

A
Granny's Puzzle
Cut 96

Granny's Puzzle by Mary Hickey, 1989, Seattle, Washington, 24" x 33". The numerous triangles in this design appear to form squares but, at the next moment, split into stars. Narrow sashings made of the background fabric separate the blocks and eliminate the need to match the points of the triangles as the quilt top is assembled.

E
Granny's Puzzle
Set Piece Cut 17

← Straight of grain →

G
Granny's Puzzle
Sashing Cut 4

¼" seam allowance

F

Granny's Puzzle
Sashing
Cut 14

Swallow's Nest

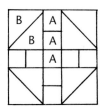

Quilt: 19½" x 26½"
Block: 5" x 5"
6 blocks

Materials: 44"-wide fabric

½ yd. brown for small triangles and outer borders
¼ yd. rose for small squares and inner borders
¼ yd. muslin for background in blocks
½ yd. tan for small squares and large set pieces
⅝ yd. backing fabric
Batting, binding, and thread

Cutting

All measurements include ¼"-wide seam allowances.
From the brown, cut:
    24 Template B
    4 strips, each 2" x 24", for outer border
From the rose, cut:
    24 Template A
    4 strips, each 1½" x 22", for inner border
From the muslin, cut:
    24 Template A
    24 Template B
From the tan, cut:
    6 Template A
    2 Template X for set squares (page 23)
    6 Template Y for side triangles (page 23)
    4 Template Z for corner triangles (page 23)

Directions

1. Piece the 6 blocks as shown.

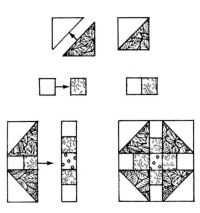

2. Sew the blocks in diagonal rows as shown.

3. Sew the rows together to form the quilt top.
4. When blocks are sewn in diagonal rows, the bias pull on the blocks and set pieces can cause them to change fractionally. For this reason, the borders are cut slightly longer than necessary and trimmed to fit the quilt. Measure the length of the quilt at the center and trim 2 of the rose border strips to that measurement. Sew these strips to the sides of the quilt, easing or stretching as necessary.
5. Measure the width of the quilt at the center and trim 2 of the rose strips to that measurement. Sew these strips to the top and bottom of the quilt, easing or stretching as necessary.
6. Measure the length of the quilt at the center and trim 2 of the brown strips to that measurement. Sew these strips to the sides of the quilt.
7. Measure the width of the quilt at the center and trim 2 of the brown strips to that measurement. Sew these strips to the top and bottom of the quilt.
8. Layer with batting and backing.
9. Baste, quilt, and bind.

Swallow's Nest by Mary Hickey, 1990, Seattle, Washington, 19½" x 26½". The warm browns and soft roses of this beloved, old pattern capture the flavor of the eighteenth century.

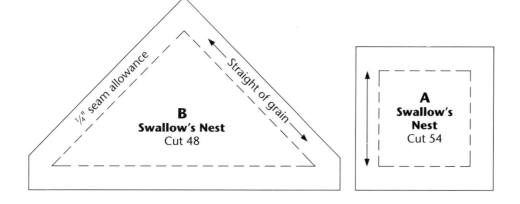

¼" seam allowance

Straight of grain

B
Swallow's Nest
Cut 48

A
Swallow's Nest
Cut 54

Slapping Prudie

by Mary Hickey

"I hit her, Julie, I just hit her. I didn't mean to. I just couldn't stop myself. She kept laughing at me with her little piggy eyes and pointing her fat finger at my shoes and giggling with her horrid laugh. She had this glob of grape jam on her collar. And then, she said something about Peter walking like a camel and I just whacked her," I cried. "Mama told me not to fight with her and now I slapped her. What am I going to do?"

"If only Mama knew how Prudence torments us. Still, she is Colonel Nangle's daughter and Mama has to work for him." My older sister was trying to be kind, but she was worried too. I sat fretting over my quilt blocks while she gazed out at the barren hillside.

"You have to tell Mama yourself, Mandy. If she hears it from you first, she can apologize to the Colonel before he says anything about it." Julie was always good and she never fought with anyone.

I felt my stomach tighten. I didn't want to tell Mama, but I knew Julie was right.

Handing me a bunch of carrots, Julie started peeling and slicing potatoes. Her red hair curled over her shoulders. The late October sun glared in through the kitchen window, adding to my irritation as I chopped the carrots.

"I wish these carrots were Prudie's patent leather shoes," I said, whacking them with all my might.

"I wish these potatoes were that purple satin dress that she wore to school on recitation day," Julie laughed.

"Remember the day she hid Miss Nelson's grade book? And the time she put a lizard in Miss Koerner's hat?" I had to admit Prudie was funny sometimes. I just hated it when she was funny at my expense—and at Peter's. And now I had slapped her, and Mama might lose her job all because of me.

Julie and I hurried supper onto the stove. John and Peter brought in the wood they had been collecting along the railroad track. John's shirt sleeves were too short, and his freckled wrists showed for three inches beyond the cuffs. Peter had a brown smudge on his cheek. They dropped the wood next to the stove and dashed back out to bring in water for washing up.

"I hear you pasted Prudie a good one," John shouted as he slammed the door.

"Oh no!" I wailed. "I'll bet it's all over town and Mama already knows. I wish I had just kept my temper like Mama said." But then I thought about Prudie making fun of the way Peter walks, and I remembered the way her cheek felt when I slapped it and the shocked look on her face, and I realized it felt good.

The boys were dancing around the stove like vultures over a stray lamb. John kept sticking his finger in the stew and licking it, and Peter kept picking off the edges of the muffins.

"I wonder why Mama is so late," Julie worried.

We waited, hungry and unsettled. John and Julie opened their books and started on their homework. John was fourteen and Julie twelve and they were both perfect. I was ten and made a muddle of everything. I was too anxious to study. I could already see the hurt in Mama's eyes when she found out I had lost my temper again and slapped the boss's daughter. Mama was the bookkeeper for Colonel Nangle's Big Washoe Mine.

Suddenly, the back door swung open and Mama bustled in.

"Oh gracious, what a day I've had," Mama said all in a rush. "Peter and John, go wash your faces. Julia, start dishing up the stew.

"Colonel and Mrs. Nangle are giving a ball

next Saturday," she added. "Mrs. Nangle wanted printed invitations but couldn't write up the words herself or take them to the printer."

Mama could give orders and carry on a conversation at the same time. "Amanda, pour the milk in the cups. Then she said only my tea cakes would do for her ball guests and ordered two hundred fifty of them. Peter, put a napkin in your collar. She wants you girls to help serve at the ball, and she'll pay John and Peter to help people with their wraps when they get to the mine."

"The mine!" Peter and I interrupted in unison. "A ball in the mine?"

"Yes, the underground station in the Big Washoe," Mama said.

Colonel Nangle's mine had a station 1040 feet underground. With an area 30 feet square and 34 feet high, it was the largest mine station in Virginia City. The mine cage could take eight people at once, down into the station.

Forgetting all about my crime, we chattered about the underground ball and our part in it.

1875 was a bonanza year in our town. A new layer of pure silver 54 feet wide had been discovered under Mount Davidson. It had to be the most inconvenient place anyone could imagine to find gold and silver. High in the Nevada desert, the place was cold in winter, sweltering in summer, and dry and windy all the time. No trees, no water, and no roads. But the magic of gold and silver had drawn people, and they had made a fancy city here in the middle of the wind and sagebrush. We had a five-story hotel, an opera house, and a railroad. Mark Twain lived here and wrote for the newspaper. We even had camels in our town because some haulers used them as pack animals. The mine owners had their clothes made in Paris and their chefs came from Vienna.

Life in Virginia City was rougher for our family than for the richer folks, but it was still interesting and exciting—except when Prudie Nangle mocked our hand-me-down clothes and Peter's limp.

Papa had died in a mine fire the year after Peter was born. Mama was educated and good with numbers so she was able to get a job as a bookkeeper for Colonel Nangle. With four children, however, the money she made barely cov-

ered our rent, and we had learned to sew and bake, to collect wood, and to do errands to earn extra money. We had never seen a ball. The thought of hearing the music and seeing all the ladies' beautiful dresses was thrilling.

"We'll have to charge the flour and sugar at Stewart's General Store," Mama said, sighing. She hated to charge anything.

"You girls can cook beets for supper tomorrow and save the juice. We'll simmer it after supper to make the pink dye for the frosting," Mama said.

"Julia, you can start making butter tomorrow. And Mandy, I want you to go to Mrs. Korslund's cook and ask to borrow their cake molds," said Mama.

Mama did not see Julie look sadly at the red box we had hidden under the daybed. The little quilt Julie and I were working on for Mama's birthday lay hidden in the folds of clean tissue in the box. The tiny triangles and squares cut from scraps of our dresses had to wait until after the ball. Nor did Julie notice Mama's dismayed glance at the big Quail's Nest quilt in the frame. Mama loved to quilt. She toiled during the day working for other people, and she felt she just had to have a few minutes each day to create something beautiful and lasting.

Two hundred fifty tea cakes meant we would have to work constantly for the next few days: buying ingredients, making the cakes, and preparing the tiny sugar roses to place on top of each cake. The boys would have to scour the countryside for enough wood to keep our old stove at the right temperature for the continual baking. But Mama would be paid in cash and we could breathe easier for a few weeks.

"Mama," I said trying to bring up the subject of the slap.

"Oh, Amanda, I forgot. You'll have to wear Julia's red cotton dress. It's too small for her. John and Peter can wear their white shirts. I don't know what on earth Julia will wear."

I looked at Julie helplessly. She smiled and shrugged her shoulders.

I didn't manage to confess my scrap with Prudie that night or all that week. The crime sat in the back of my mind haunting my every waking moment. I knew that Mama would hear about it once the excitement of the ball passed.

Such a frenzy of preparations for the ball! In Strainer's Pharmacy, Yenter's Dry Goods, and McKinney's Mercantile, everyone discussed the underground ball—who was invited and who was not, what Mrs. Baker would wear, how Mrs. McAuliffe would do her red hair, and when Mrs. Epler would arrive. At school, Prudie kept her distance but pointed at me and whispered mocking words to her giggling followers.

After school, we hunted for wood; churned butter; and measured sugar, flour, baking powder, and nutmeg into jars. John and Peter cleaned out the fire box inside the stove. In Virginia City, where wood was scarce, we had to protect our scant supply from theft by storing it in the house, stacked under the quilt frame.

"We'll bake fifty cakes Thursday evening and fifty Friday night. We dare not use the stove too late at night or sparks from the chimney might catch in the stronger nighttime zephyrs," said Mama as she hemmed the dress she was making over for Julie. The dry winds, or zephyrs as we called them, combined with the scarcity of water, made fire a constant menace in Virginia City.

"We should be able to bake the last hundred and fifty cakes on Saturday without any problem," Julie said.

Holding up the dress she had just completed, Mama said, "This royal blue will look pretty on you, Julia. And when this ball is behind us, we can go back to piecing the new quilt for the boys' bed and quilting the one in the frame."

By six o'clock Saturday we stood awkwardly in the mine office, all scrubbed and clothed in our made-over hand-me-downs. Two hundred fifty pink tea cakes sat regally on Mrs. Nangle's grand silver trays.

"I want each of you to carry a tray of cakes down with you in the mine cage. Once you reach the station, you must stay in the area of the ball because the tunnels are dangerous while the miners are working," Mama said, handing John a tray.

"You mean the miners are going to be working during the ball?" I asked.

"Sure, the mine operates twenty-four hours a day," said Peter who was fascinated by mining and machinery. "They have too much equipment down there to let it sit idle. There are over three hundred miles of tunnels shored up by honeycombed timbers and a narrow-gauge railroad and a telegraph system between each level. The hoisting cage that will take us down can lift six tons of ore."

"Just be sure that you don't leave the station area. You could get lost in those tunnels," Mama cautioned, looking sternly at Peter.

"Send those kids down with the food," barked Colonel Nangle, coming up behind Mama in the mine office.

My arms trembled as I stepped into the hoist cage.

"Lean up against them posts," Emmett Lynch shouted as he yanked the starting lever.

My stomach lurched as the cage plunged a thousand feet under the earth to the main station of the mine. A man in a butler's uniform opened the cage gate and pointed to the tables for the cakes. Boxes of sandwiches, barrels of wine and whiskey, urns of flowers, and tables set with linen and silver all decorated the underground station. I could hear the orchestra warming up in a grotto carved into the rock. Through the silver decorations, we could see the tunnels leading off from the station like spokes from a wheel. Deep in one of the tunnels, I could see men swinging picks. Their backs glistened with sweat even though in the heat they wore only red long johns. Bits of silver sparkled in the rock walls. The shrill sound of the orchestra, the crashing din of the pick axes and drills, the roar of the ore-car wheels on the tracks in the tunnels, and the whooshing sound of air being blown in to ventilate the mine combined to create a confusing din. Julie and I tried to concentrate on helping Mama arrange food and flowers among the silver on the tables, but I couldn't help staring at the wondrous sights.

"The guests will be arriving in about fifteen minutes, Mandy, so hurry and help Edna pour these juices into the punch bowls. Mildred and

Julie can start arranging the silver on that table over by the orchestra," said Mama. Edna and Mildred served as maids in the Nangle home.

"Look, Mama, they put a wood floor over the rocks," said Julie, who was fanning napkins around a silver punch bowl.

"They need to have a smooth floor to dance," Mama said as she deftly arranged oysters on the filigreed edges of a silver tray.

"Oysters!" said John, staring. "Where did they get oysters?"

"Colonel Nangle had clams and oysters brought in on the Virginia and Truckee Railroad this afternoon," explained Mama.

The hoist gate clattered. Colonel and Mrs. Nangle and Prudie stepped into the station. Prudie's dress was a pale green fluff of ruffles and ribbons. She hitched her skirt up and strutted over to the trays of pink cakes. Her green satin slippers shone in the light of the candles. My brown lace-up shoes felt heavy and grimy.

"Oh, look at these cute little cakes. I think I'll taste one." She took a bite, made a face, and dropped the rest of the cake on the dance floor. A little smudge of frosting stuck to her chin. Mrs. Nangle rolled her eyes to the ceiling. Colonel Nangle scowled at Prudie but barked at Peter and John to move two wooden coat racks into position near the mine hoist. Mama bit her lower lip and shook her head. She smoothed her hair, tucking the stray curls into the soft, red bun on top of her head.

Julie looked at me uneasily.

"Don't worry. I won't bother the little darling," I said innocently.

Mama said, "Oh look, the guests are starting to arrive. John and Peter, go offer to take their wraps."

More and more guests arrived in the mine hoist. Then, all at once, a group seemed to appear out of the rock wall!

"Look, Peter. They just came out of the stone!" I gasped.

"No, those are the people coming from Dayton on the other side of the mountain. They came on a rail car through the Sutro Tunnel," Peter informed me.

"What tunnel?" I asked.

"It's a huge tunnel designed to drain under-ground water and connect all the mine tunnels under Mount Davidson."

"How do you know all this?" I asked suspiciously.

"I've been down here before. Don't tell Mama, but Donny Murphy and I snuck in one of the openings of the Sutro tunnel. There's one right down the hill from Colonel Nangle's mansion, just behind his carriage house. We kind of got lost. But then we realized that those big gray tubes were only in the Sutro Tunnel, not in the mining tunnels. So we followed the tubes till we found a way out."

"What gray tubes?" I asked. Peter led me to an opening in the wall at the far end of the dance platform.

"See, up there," he pointed to what looked like miles of gray tubing extending along a wide tunnel. I shivered, thinking of the three hundred miles of twisting tunnels here under the mountain.

"Mandy, come help pour the punch," Julie called.

"Yes, I'm thirsty. And you're supposed to serve me," whined Prudie, coming up behind me. Her yellow sausage curls jiggled as she pranced over to the punch table.

I handed Prudie a crystal cup of pink punch. She took a gulp. A few drops dribbled on the ruffles under her chin, making a dark pink stain on the green satin.

"Oh look, they're starting to dance," said Julie.

I gazed at the ladies dressed in satin gowns and sparkling jewels and at the men clothed in crisp, long-tailed tuxedos. The orchestra started a waltz, and the candle-lit mine station was transformed into a whirl of swishing rainbows and spinning glitter. I watched Mr. Urqhart's coattails swing like the flapping wings of a crow as he danced. Mrs. Cutler's daffodil satin dress shimmered, and her diamonds glinted against the dark stone walls of the mine. Behind her in the tunnel, I could see two miners leaning over a bucket, gulping cold water. Mrs. Stanfield had three pale pink roses and tiny pearls twisted in her shining brown hair. Elegant groups sat gossiping at linen-covered tables while the miners' pick axes clanged in the distance. And all evening, the orchestra played the lovely Strauss waltzes.

I was thrilled by the beautiful music and the graceful dancing. But after four hours of pouring punch and stacking sandwiches, my arms and legs ached. At midnight, the orchestra stopped. John and Peter started handing guests their coats and furs, and the mine hoist whooshed up and down, taking guests up to Nangles' house for a champagne supper.

"You girls take the cake trays home with you to wash. Edna and Mildred and I will have to take the rest of this over to Nangles' and help with the supper," said Mama. Her skin looked gray with fatigue.

"I thought it was a beautiful ball," said Julie as we walked the eight blocks downhill toward home. "I loved hearing the orchestra play The Blue Danube Waltz."

"I liked seeing the pumps of the roof blowers forcing air through the tunnels." That was Peter, of course.

John didn't say anything but I knew he liked seeing Nan Ellis dancing in her pale blue gown. She caught him staring at her and had smiled and fluttered her fan at him.

I don't remember getting home or getting ready for bed. I just recall pulling up the beautiful Meadowlark quilt on our bed. The triangles reminded me of the swirling dancers.

Monday, after school, Julie and I ran home together to finish piecing the little quilt we were sewing for Mama's birthday.

"Look, there's a note on the table," Julie said. "Oh, Mama says you're to take the silver trays back to Nangles'."

"And you have to go up to Nollettes' and mind the twins," I read over her shoulder. "How are we ever going to finish Mama's quilt in time?" I moaned.

"You'll have to take the finished blocks with you and stop at Yenter's Dry Goods after you go to Nangles'. That way, you can pick out the border fabric. Don't worry. All we have to do is sew the last two blocks, and I'll take those with me to finish,"   Julie said smiling. "We'll have it done by Friday."

Julie grabbed her red sweater and ran up the hill

toward Nollettes'. I tucked the completed quilt blocks in my coat pocket, picked up the ornate trays, and trudged downhill toward Nangles'.

Prudie answered the door. She had a smear of lemon cream on her sleeve. She tilted her head back, flounced her tight curls, and said, "Don't you know servants are supposed to use the side door?" She slammed the door in my face.

I walked with slow fury across the porch and around to the kitchen door.

"Edna and Mildred have the day off because they worked Saturday night, so you'll have to put them away in the silver cabinet yourself," she snapped as she opened the door. Just at that moment, a look of horror crossed her face. I turned to see flames shooting above C Street and Yenter's Dry Goods, about two blocks uphill. Alarm bells clanged and sirens wailed.

"The town's on fire!" she screamed, grabbing my wrist. The dry air and lack of water in the desert, the stacks of lumber ready to shore up the mine tunnels, the stock of dynamite in the mine headquarters, and the constant howling winds were turning Virginia City into an inferno.

We both stared in terror at the flames flashing from roof to roof. As the air became heated, whole blocks seemed to blaze up at once. Standing in the street next to Nangles' mansion, we could see people streaming out of the center of town to escape the smoke and flames. We stood gripping hands, paralyzed at the sound of whole cases of blasting powder exploding. The fierce winds forced the fire through the city, hurling sheets of flaming debris through the air.

Firemen attached hoses, and engines began to pump water on the flames. They might as well have tried to quench a volcano. Sparks rained onto the roof of the porch.

"Run!" I screamed as flames licked up the walls of the Nangle mansion.

Prudie was still gripping my hand. We ran downhill to escape the advancing blaze, but the flames had leaped over us and we were racing directly into more fire.

"We're trapped!" Prudie shrieked. Sparks pricked our arms and cheeks.

Whirling smoke stung our eyes.

"This way, hurry!" I yelled. Yanking her hand, I dragged Prudie after me through the hail of hot cinders toward the back of their carriage house to the opening of the Sutro Tunnel.

"In here!" I screamed. "Help me slam the doors." It took both of us to push the huge metal doors shut against hot blasts of wind. A terrifying crash echoed through the tunnel as flaming rubbish bombarded the doors.

We ran, stumbling in the sudden blackness, away from the heat of the doors. At last, gasping, we collapsed onto the damp floor.

"Where are we?" Prudie asked in a small panting voice.

"I'm not sure," I said, trembling in the darkness.

"How did you know about this place?" Her voice sounded different.

"My brother Peter told me about it. We're in some sort of tunnel," I said.

To my shock, she said, "You are so lucky to have a brother like Peter."

"I thought you hated him. I thought you hated all of us."

"I only hated you because you have everything," she said, sniffing.

"We have everything? You're the one who's rich and wears patent leather shoes," I said, startled.

"You're the one who is smart and has a mother who likes you. You're the one who has brothers and a sister to talk to!"

I sat in stunned disbelief. Finally, Prudie asked, "How do we get out of here?"

"I can't remember. Something about pipes," I said, trying to recall Peter's words.

"I can feel a pipe up above me," said Prudie.

Standing on tiptoe, I felt the pipe.

"Gray tubes," I said. "Peter said the Sutro Tunnel had a large gray tube running all through it. He and Donny followed the tubes until they found their way out."

"I stumbled on a stick just before we sat down," Prudie said. "If we could find it, we could

hold it up and use it to reach the tubes and tell if we are following them."

I was amazed. "That's a great idea," I said.

After a few minutes of groping around, we found the stick and started on our slow walk through the dark tunnel. When we came to a cross tunnel, we held hands tightly and tapped the upper parts of the walls till we found the pipes. After about half an hour of groping, we came to a lighted area.

"Where in tarnation did you come from?" asked a startled voice.

A team of miners were standing in a grotto, holding a lantern. When we explained that we had come into the mine to escape the surrounding fire, they looked troubled.

"The hoisting mechanisms are all burned, and we haven't figured how we're gettin' out."

"We can go out through the Sutro Tunnel to Dayton on the other side of the mountain," I suggested.

"Gosh darn, I think she's right. But that's a long way," said one of the men.

"We can hitch a mule to an ore car and ride," offered another man.

It took about two hours to get to the opening at Dayton. And another three hours before Mama and the Nangles realized we were alive.

Two thousand buildings in our town had burned to the ground that Monday afternoon in October. By Tuesday, the Virginia and Truckee Railroad was hauling in lumber for rebuilding. Relief boxes poured into Virginia City from all over the West.

We had to stay with friends in Gold Hill for about five weeks. We lost all our big quilts, but Colonel Nangle helped Mama rebuild our house. Julie and I still had the blocks for Mama's gift quilt in our pockets. Mama hung that little quilt over the doorway in our rebuilt house.

Mama never did hear about my fight, but over the years, sitting around the quilting frame, Prudie and I often told Mama every detail of our hand-in-hand race to the tunnel and our walk through the dark mine.

Zephyr

Quilt: 25" x 25"
Block: 4½" x 4½"
16 blocks

Materials: 44"-wide fabric

¼ yd. assorted dark prints for triangles
¼ yd. assorted medium prints for squares
¼ yd. assorted light prints for triangles and squares
⅛ yd. red for inner border fabric
¼ yd. blue for outer border fabric
¾ yd. backing fabric
Batting, binding, and thread

Cutting

All measurements include ¼"-wide seam allowances.
From the assorted dark fabrics, cut:
    64 Template B
From the assorted medium fabrics, cut:
    32 Template A
From the assorted light fabrics, cut:
    48 Template A
    64 Template B
From the inner border fabric, cut:
    2 strips, each 1¼" x 18½", for the side borders
    2 strips, each 1¼" x 20", for the top and bottom borders
From the outer border fabric, cut:
    2 strips, each 3" x 20", for the side borders
    2 strips, each 3" x 25", for the top and bottom borders

Directions

1. Piece 16 blocks as shown.

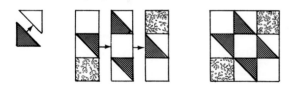

2. Arrange the blocks in rows as shown. Notice that each block is given a quarter turn from the block next to it.

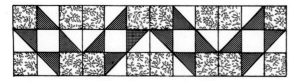

3. Matching the corners and triangles, sew the blocks together in rows of 4.
4. Again matching the corners and triangles, sew the rows together to form the quilt top.
5. Stitch the inner borders to the quilt, sides first, then the top and bottom.
6. Sew the outer borders to the quilt, sides first, then the top and bottom.
7. Layer with batting and backing.
8. Baste, quilt, and bind.

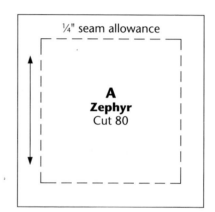

¼" seam allowance

A
Zephyr
Cut 80

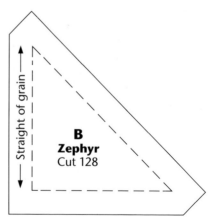

Straight of grain

B
Zephyr
Cut 128

Zephyr by Mary Hickey, 1991, Seattle, Washington, 25" x 25". Unpretentious blocks, sprinkled with dark triangles amid the dominant lights and mediums and rotated a quarter turn, make this quilt an intriguing puzzle.

Fluttering Fans

Quilt: 26⅝" x 26⅝"
Block: 4½" x 4½"
13 blocks

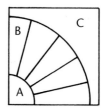

Materials: 44"-wide fabric

½ yd. blue for border and base of fans
⅛ yd. yellow for inner border
¼ yd. assorted yellows for fans
½ yd. light print for background in blocks and set triangles
¾ yd. backing fabric
Batting, binding, and thread

Cutting

All measurements include ¼"-wide seam allowances.
From the blue for base of fans and outer border, cut:

13 Template A
2 strips, each 3" x 21⅝", for side borders
2 strips, each 3" x 26⅝", for top and bottom borders

From the yellow inner border fabric, cut:

2 strips, each 1½" x 19⅛", for side borders
2 strips, each 1½" x 21⅝", for top and bottom borders

From the assorted yellows, cut:

65 Template B

From the light print for background and set triangles, cut:

13 Template C
8 Template D
4 Template E

Directions

1. Piece 13 fan sections as shown, using 5 pieces in each fan. Sew a line of basting stitches along the narrow end of the fan ⅛" from the raw edge.

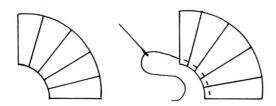

2. Pin a Template C piece to the top (wide section) of each fan. Start by pinning each end and then pin the center. Insert 3 or 4 more pins to ease the fullness of the Template C piece. Machine stitch with the Template C section on top.

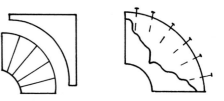

3. Using Template A-1, make 13 heavy-paper templates.

4. Machine baste the corners of the blue fabric cut from Template A to the heavy paper as shown.

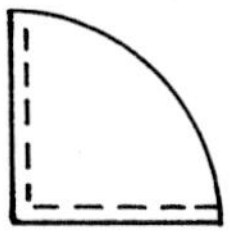

5. Hand sew a line of stitching ⅛" from the curved edge of the blue fabric. Pull on the hand-basting thread and gather the fabric around the template. The fabric will be smooth on the front of the template and gathered only on the underside.

6. Appliqué a blue fan base to the bottom curved edge of each fan. If the fan does not quite fit the base, pull on the basting stitches in the fan, easing it to fit the base.

7. Arrange the blocks and set triangles in diagonal rows as shown.

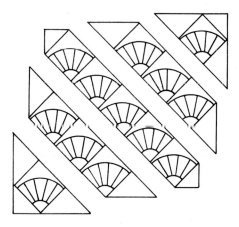

8. Sew the blocks and triangles into diagonal rows.
9. Sew the rows together to form the quilt top.
10. Stitch the inner borders to the quilt, sides first, then the top and bottom, easing or stretching to fit as necessary.
11. Stitch the outer borders to the quilt, sides first, then the top and bottom, easing or stretching to fit as necessary.
12. Layer with batting and backing.
13. Baste, quilt, and bind.

Fluttering Fans by Cleo Nollette, 1991, Seattle, Washington, 26⅝" x 26⅝". Fans for moving the sultry summer air or hiding shy smiles were a favorite design for early quilters. In this cheerful interpretation, Cleo's simple arrangement forms a lovely graphic image.

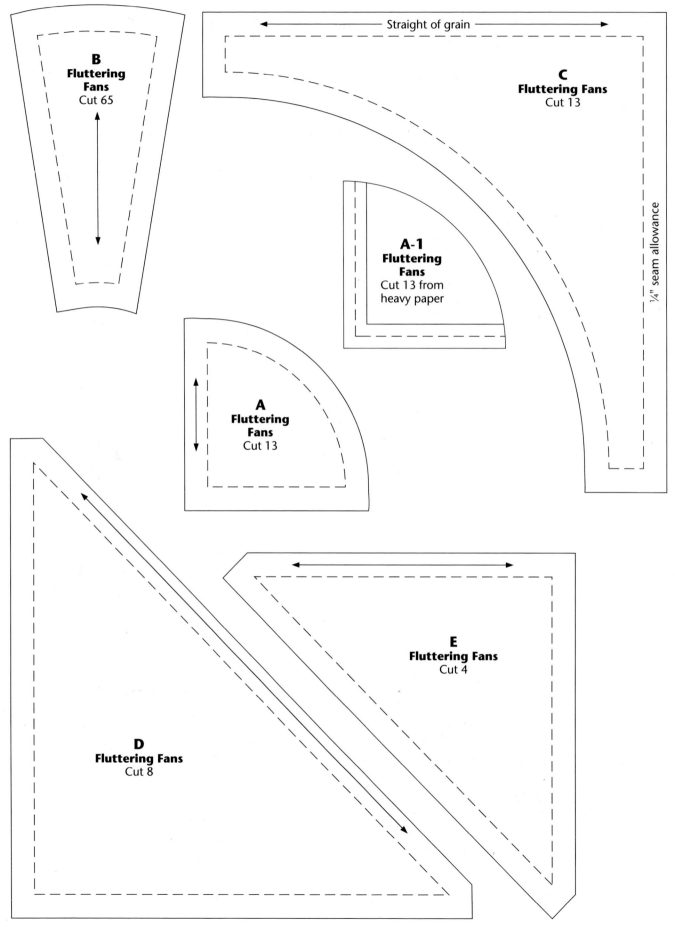

B
Fluttering Fans
Cut 65

Straight of grain

C
Fluttering Fans
Cut 13

¼" seam allowance

A-1
Fluttering Fans
Cut 13 from heavy paper

A
Fluttering Fans
Cut 13

E
Fluttering Fans
Cut 4

D
Fluttering Fans
Cut 8

Finishing a Quilt

Adding Borders

Small works of art are greatly enhanced by careful framing. Thoughtfully planned and sewn borders function as frames for quilt designs. You will find a variety of border designs in *Pioneer Storybook Quilts*. Take some time to study the elements of the borders. Multiple strips of fabric are sewn together for the border of Pioneer Pinwheels (page 20), and a striped fabric adds pizzazz to Magic Trees (page 38).

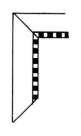

Floral or paisley stripes make wonderful borders, as in Rocky Mountain Stars (page 40).

If you prefer a different treatment for your quilt from the one pictured, simply find the border design you prefer in a different quilt plan and change the measurements to fit your quilt.

However you compose your border, you must decide whether to sew the corners with straight-cut and-sewn seams or with mitered corners. For straight-sewn corners, first sew the borders to the long sides of the quilt and then to the shorter sides. Mitered corners are not difficult to make and are worth the added effort in many designs.

The fabric requirements in the quilt plans include border requirements and allow a few extra inches for shrinkage. Cut border strips about 2" longer than the length of the quilt. Before you sew the borders to the quilt top, trim them to fit.

Straight-Sewn Corners

1. Measure the length of the quilt in the center by folding the quilt in half lengthwise and measuring the folded edge. Note this number.

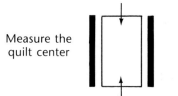

Measure the quilt center

2. Cut the inner side borders to this measurement.
3. Stitch the inner borders to the quilt top. Ease or stretch the quilt top to fit the border strips. By forcing the quilt to fit the measured strips, your finished quilt will be square, with flat borders. This is an important step, so resist the temptation to skip it by just sewing the unmeasured strips to the sides. You certainly don't want baggy borders, do you?

4. Measure the width of the quilt by folding the quilt in half crosswise and measuring the width along the fold, including the side borders. Note this measurement.

5. Cut the inner top and bottom borders to this measurement.
6. Sew the inner borders to the top and bottom, easing or stretching to fit the quilt to the borders.
7. Repeat this process for the middle and outer borders.

Mitered Corners

1. Measure your quilt top and calculate the finished outside dimensions of the quilt, including the borders.
2. Cut the border strips 2" longer than the outer measurements of the quilt. Trim any excess fabric after you have sewn the mitered corner.
3. If you are using multiple borders, center the strips on each other and sew them together, creating striped fabric that can be treated as one unit.
4. Center the strips of border fabric on the sides of the quilt top.
5. Start stitching the borders to the quilt top ¼" from one end of the quilt and stop ¼" from the other end. Stitch the four borders to the quilt, always leaving the first and last ¼" unsewn.

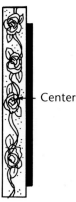

Center

6. Arrange the quilt with one corner right side up on the ironing board.
7. Fold one border into a 45° angle with the other border. Work with the stripes so they meet. With the heads of the pins all facing the center of the quilt, pin the fold; press.

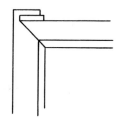

8. Use 1" masking tape to hold the mitered angle in place. Start at the outer edge of the quilt and carefully center the tape over the mitered fold as you remove the pins.

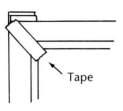

Tape

9. Turn the quilt over and draw a light pencil line on the crease created by pressing in step 7.
10. Stitch on the pencil line and remove the tape.
11. Trim away the excess fabric.
12. Repeat steps 6–10 on the remaining corners.

Marking

Carefully press the quilt top and trace the quilting designs onto it. (See pages 78–80 for some suggested quilting patterns.) Use a sharp pencil and mark lightly. If you prefer to use a water-soluble pen, test for removability on a scrap before marking the quilt. Chalk dispensers and white pencils are available to mark dark fabrics. Or, you may mark the quilt top for straight-line quilting with ¼" masking tape after the quilt is basted.

Backing

Make a quilt backing that is 1" larger than your quilt top. Spread the backing, wrong side up, over a clean, flat surface. Use masking tape to anchor the backing to the surface without stretching it.

Batting

Batting is the filler between the backing and the quilt top. A lightweight cotton/polyester (80%/20%) combination batting works well. Battings of 100% cotton are also excellent but must be closely quilted to prevent shifting during laundering. Less quilting is needed with a 100% polyester bonded batting. However, some polyester may creep through the fabric and create tiny "beards" on the surface of the quilt. This problem usually occurs only on dark fabrics. For most doll quilts, I use a lightweight bonded polyester batting.

Basting

Spread the quilt batting over the backing, making sure it covers the entire backing and is smooth. Center the pressed and marked quilt top, right side up, over the batting. Align the borders and straight lines with the edges of the backing and pin-baste the layers together carefully.

Baste the three layers together, using a long needle and light-colored quilting thread. If you thread your needle without cutting the thread off the spool, you will be able to baste at least one long row without rethreading your needle. Starting at the center of the quilt, use large stitches to baste an X on the quilt from corner to corner.

Continue basting, creating a grid of parallel lines 3"–5" apart. Complete the basting with a line of careful stitches around the outside edges.

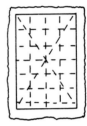

Quilting

Quilting is simply a short running stitch with a single thread that goes through all three quilt layers.

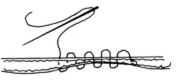

Quilt on a frame, in a hoop, on a table top, or on your lap. Use quilting thread; it is thicker and less likely to tangle. Use a short, fine (#10 or #12) needle to take small stitches. Cut the thread 20" long and tie a small knot. Starting about 1" from where you want the quilting to begin, insert the needle through the top and batting only. Gently tug on the knot until it pops through the quilt top and is caught in the batting. Take small, even, straight stitches through all layers.

To make small stitches, push the needle with a thimble on your middle finger. Insert the needle and push it straight down. Then, rock the needle up and down through all layers, "loading" three or four stitches on the needle. Pull the needle through, aiming toward yourself as you work. Place your other hand under the quilt and use your thumbnail to make sure the needle has penetrated all three layers with each stitch.

To end a line of quilting, make a single knot close to the quilt top and then take a 1" stitch through the top and batting only. Pull the knot through the fabric into the batting. Clip the thread at the surface of the quilt. When all the quilting is completed, remove the basting, except for the stitches around the edges. What a joyous moment this is!

Binding

Trim the batting and backing even with the quilt top. Cut 2"-wide bias strips from the binding fabric. Seam the bias strips, end to end, to make a strip that is long enough to go all the way around the quilt plus about 3". Turn under a ½"-wide hem on one long edge of the binding and press, being careful not to stretch the bias.

Starting just to the right of the center on one side and with the front of the quilt facing you, place the raw, unpressed edge of the binding on the edge of the quilt. Sew the binding to the quilt front, using ¼"-wide seams. Do not pin the binding to the quilt but smooth it in place, about 3" at a time, without stretching it.

Stop your stitching ¼" from the end of the quilt at the first corner and backtack.

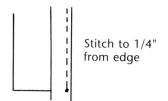

Stitch to 1/4" from edge

Remove the quilt from the sewing machine. Push a pin from the back of the quilt up through your stitching line and ¼" from the edge of the quilt. Fold the binding, creating a 45° angle. The binding should form a straight line out from the side of the quilt that will be sewn next.

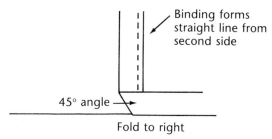

Binding forms straight line from second side

45° angle

Fold to right

Hold the fold down with your finger and fold the rest of the binding back over itself to the edge that will be sewn next.

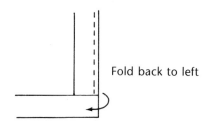

Fold back to left

Push a pin up through the very edge of the fold; start stitching at the point where the pin comes up through the binding (¼" from the corner).

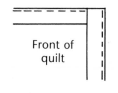

Front of quilt

Continue around all four sides and corners of your quilt in the same manner. Fold under the raw edge of the binding when you reach the starting point.

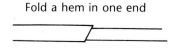

Fold a hem in one end

When the binding is all stitched, place your finger under one of the corners and push the fold toward the point. Fold the fabric around to the back of the quilt and fold a miter on the back of the corner. Complete all four corners this way. Whipstitch the binding by hand onto the back of the quilt.

Back of quilt

Front of quilt after folding binding to back

Labeling

Labeling your quilt is an important finishing touch. You can embroider or cross-stitch your name, city, and the date on the back of your quilt. If you have too much information to stitch, you can letter a label with a permanent pen on muslin, or type the information on muslin and stitch it to the back.

Molly Hickey
Seattle, Wa
1991

Suggested Quilting Patterns

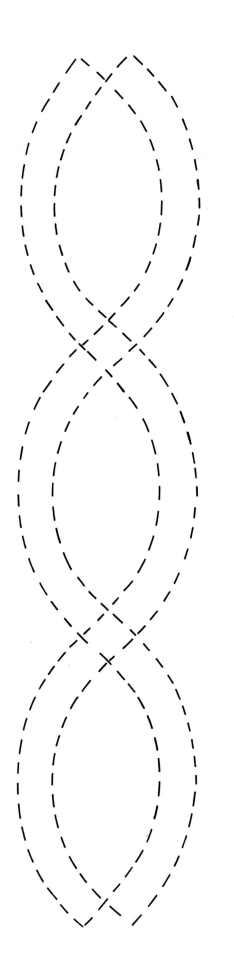
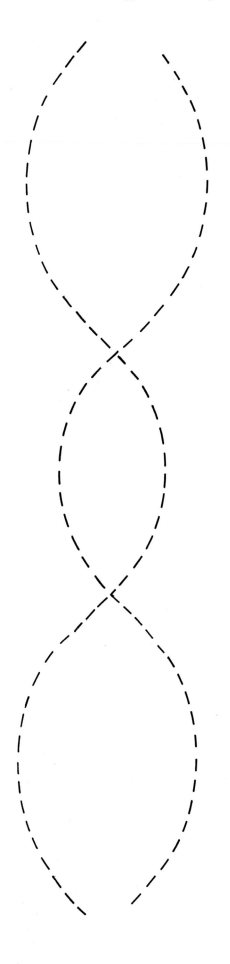